ZAWIA DISCOURSES

Etsko Schuitema

INTENT PUBLISHING

About our logo:

The square in the middle represents The One. From The One, come the two surrounding lines, the 'Outward' and the 'Inward'. The next four are the 'Sensory' and 'Meaning' aspects of the 'Inward' and 'Outward', and the last eight the 'Celestial' and 'Terrestrial' manifestations of the previous aspects.

CONTENTS

Chapter 1

THE PARENT OF ALL VIRTUES
Discourse 1: 27 April 2013

Bismillah ar-rahman ar-raheem

The first virtue, the parent of all virtues, is gratitude. Why this should be the case becomes apparent when you consider the opposite. The first vice, the parent of all vices, is ingratitude and resentment. If I am convinced that the world has done me in and that what I have received is not good enough, then I feel in some measure short-changed. Then it is legitimate for me to act in pursuit of my own interests and to defend myself. Then I am of the view that since life has been unjust to me, I cannot trust life. It means I have to look after my own interests and, in the process, I justify what I do to others and what I do to the world.

Contrary to this, if I am convinced that I have received in excess of my due, then I know that the generous hand and the generous Lord, who has given me in excess of my due, will continue to give me in excess, which means I don't have to look after myself. I don't have to look after number one because Rabb al-'aalameen looks after me. As Imam Kamardine recited from the Qur'an, Allah SWT is the best of providers.

This is particularly important to us today because, as Muslims in this age, it is very easy to develop a narrative of victimhood. They are bombing our people in Afghanistan, Iraq, and Pakistan. Pick up a newspaper and, all over, there is the sense that the Umma is on the back foot. We are under attack by the monster. This is a very dangerous development because this is a unique development in Islamic history. Up to 1922, we never had that sense of being under the heel, but now we are and we are outraged by it. We have so completely swallowed the moral outrage of having lost out in the ascendency of the West, that the outrage now presents itself to us as virtuous.

In our days with the Murabitun, we used to think it was absolutely acceptable to raid, to do ghazwa, and to take other people's property because we were oppressed. To rob was good. It was the justifiable act of the oppressed Muslims against the oligarchy, the Jews, and the Masons. Their property was halaal for us and to die in this endeavour was to die the death of a shaheed, the noble death of a martyr who will go straight to paradise. And many of us got killed. Although, with the benefit of hindsight, I now seriously doubt whether their assurance of paradise was as credible as we thought.

What if our protestation of victimhood was not an expression of imaan, but an expression of kufr? What if any protestation of victimhood is an affront to the one to whom we all bore witness: 'Indeed, You are our Rabb'.

Any sense that you have of being oppressed is an outrage. How can you not recognize that you are the recipient of blessings beyond calculation, no matter how oppressed you think you are. Maybe you live in a war zone. Maybe you had to battle to get through the week. But you did battle through the week and you are here.

Surely, if more things had gone wrong in your life rather than gone right, you wouldn't be here. If that were true, you would be dead. But you are not dead. Not to recognise that the sum total of the curse and the challenge of your life is always minuscule in relation to the blessing it holds is not only to misapprehend things shamelessly, but it is also an affront to your Rabb.

There is a further problem with our victim narrative. There is no imprisonment and oppression that gets exercised over us which we are not complicit in, and that's particularly true for our brotherhood and our circle. In this circle, we profess to be the adorers of Allah SWT. He gives us other human beings as a metaphor to understand our relationship with Him.

So picture this: you give a person something and that person does not recognise what you are giving to him and shows absolutely no gratitude at all. Are you likely to give anything to him a second time? Of course not. Whereas if you gave that person something and they indicated their sincere gratitude, it becomes pleasurable to give something to that person again. So too, if we are grateful to Him, He will increase us. If we show Him resentment, He will take away from us. And yet, by His stupendous mercy, He gives even to the ungrateful.

The same rules that account for your engagement with other people are actually at work between you and reality and existence, but at a far more profound level and on a much bigger scale. If you do not, in every moment, commence the moment with gratitude, with alhumdullilah, you are like the man who is given the gift and doesn't say thank you. This is for the minutest things: your breathing, your ability to talk, or your ability to sit.

We have all the tools needed to climb out of the quagmire of our bitterness and resentment, but then we have to apply the tools to that end. The practices aren't just about learning a couple of interesting phrases in Arabic. The practices are about creating a framework so that you can incrementally, step-by-step, claw your way out of the morass of your own mediocrity, of your own day-to-day dinginess. You have to understand that your resentment is an outrage against how things are.

What do you have that hasn't come from other than you? The water that courses through your veins, the breath in your lungs, the energy that allows you to do the dhikr, to walk up to the majlis, to greet the child. - where does this come from? You don't manufacture this out of your own being; it comes from other than you. So how can you look at others with a sense that it's not good enough?

We are like a conference of moles sitting in the company of a lion. We are not aware that this looming reality that is towering over us is actually tolerating us. As a consequence, we are having a mole-like dispute, carefully noting how one mole has a slightly higher heap than another. And this causes us great distress, as we squeeze our little mole behinds to bellow our squeaky outrage at the injustice of it all. But we are blind. We do not see the looming majesty.

If we saw things as they are, we would see that we are all actually very small, petty moles in the face of the lion. Maybe we wouldn't have such an argument. We would see it for how ridiculous it is, particularly once we realised that all of it, even the little inequities of the molehills, were the gifts of the lion. Rather than be disagreeable with each other, we would be grateful to the one who gave it all.

I think the moment the moles did that, the doors of blessing would open. While you are ungrateful, why should the Lord of the worlds give you anything?

When you shift how you engage with your life from resentment to gratitude, you then create the conditions where Allah SWT opens up the doors of blessing for you. A real sense of fullness is not the product of the things you own or have. Do you honestly think that a person who has a big bank account is necessarily any more secure and happy than you are? This is not so. I know many people who are very wealthy, but they are utterly miserable.

What makes the fullness is not in the object; the fullness is in being filled with gratitude; it is in appreciativeness. If you drink a glass of juice and it's just any old juice, you probably can't even work out afterwards what you drank. Was it orange or guava or mango? But if you sip that juice slowly and you let it percolate into your being so that you truly appreciate it, then you have actually drunk the juice. So without appreciativeness and without this ability to savour, it's like you don't have a life. It doesn't matter what the drink is. Without the ability to savour the drink, it is not even like water. So the critical ingredient is the savouring. It is the appreciativeness. It is the gratitude.

We are a mote of dust in the middle of this fathomless void. We are not going to be here for very long at all, and to lose even that little spot because of ingratitude is a tragedy.

May Allah SWT grant us nearness to Him,
May Allah SWT grant us annihilation in Him,
May Allah SWT grant us death before we die.

Chapter 2

REDISCOVERING OUR FULLNESS
Discourse 2: 29 September 2018

Bismillah ar-rahman ar-raheem

Much of our life is really concerned with pursuing aspiration, of going after what we want to get out of life. This goal-directed shaping of our beings is the fundamental human condition. It's what we get taught by our parents and it's the first principle that makes all human interaction, human cooperation, and language possible.

Most of how we understand the deen to be phrased is also in this context – we do things in order to get things. I do things to earn thawab. I do things to achieve a place in akhira. So, this way of orienting our aspirations and intentions is about something better in the future. That better is either on this side of the grave – we do things in business or in relationships in order to achieve a better condition – or we do things to achieve a better akhira – the other side of the grave. Our intent is forward-focused, and our aspiration is forward-focused.

It should, however, become apparent that you can look at this issue of attention and your intent from two points of view. They both have to do with how one deals with time. You either see time as unfolding into the future and your engagement with time is about achieving things that are still to come. Or you can see time as an unfolding of what has already been decreed. Now, the difference between these two is not small. The person who aspires to get things in the future is operating from a place of lack. They're saying, 'What I have is not adequate. My physical condition is not adequate. My spiritual condition is not adequate. I need to do things to get these in the future – a better future'. So you can describe the intent of this person as an emptiness that seeks to be filled. This person's aspiration is an emptiness that wants to achieve things in the world.

The other way of looking at your life is that you've already received enormously in excess of your due. There's nothing to be achieved. There's only enjoyment of what has already been granted. You can describe that person – a person who acts on the basis of a sense of fullness that overflows – as a truly free human being. A person who orientates their aspiration towards the future is saying, 'I still want to get stuff for my life'. You can describe that person as an empty human being. A person who says, 'I have already had the best and what comes from me is an overflowing' can be described as a full human being.

The peculiar truth to this is that the person who assumes that he has already received in excess of his due and he is owed no more and doesn't aspire enormously to go somewhere else – that person goes further and achieves more than the person who is trying to get stuff out of the world. This is simply because that person's being is rooted in gratitude.

We seem to think that what happens in our chest is somehow divorced from what happens in the world around us. But if my heart is full and I'm a grateful person, then when I interact with other people around me, they will experience that gratitude. And because they experience that gratitude, they will find it pleasurable to give more to me.

There's nothing that you're trying to get out of life that doesn't come from something other than you. And other than you is like a big person. If you refract it down to individual interactions, when you deal with somebody in the spirit of being owed, that person doesn't want to give you anything. But if you interact with that person in the spirit of being grateful, it's pleasurable for that person to give you something. And so it is with the whole of life.

So, take the person who goes through their life with the assumption that they've already received whatever there is to receive and that they're full. If their action is based on this fullness and overflowing, that action is, by definition, unconditional. That action is, by definition, rooted in gratitude. And, because that is the case, that action contains the biggest benefit and reward.

Bizarrely, it's precisely the person who can forgo the reward that gets the reward. A person who acts because they're still trying to get stuff out of the world is constantly contending with the world. They're constantly trying to wrestle things from life. Even for the person who constructs their life based on doing things for akhira, the great danger in that is that you walk through the world in the spirit of judgement: 'This is beneath me. This is of dunya. This is worldly'. And it doesn't matter if you're acting for akhira or for dunya, your deportment in life becomes a contending deportment. You're not in a state of peace; you're in a state of combat.

So, there are these two ways of looking at life: 'My life has lack. My life has emptiness and I act to fill it' or 'My life is full, and I act out of a spontaneous overflowing of gratitude from a fullness that is there'.

The difference between the two is not the product of action. The difference between gratitude and resentment, between fullness and emptiness, is not based on what you do; it is based on how you see things. It is something that happens behind your eyes. So, this perceptual trick of finding what there is to be grateful about, of being full – that way of seeing produces the right action. Conversely, the way of seeing which convinces you that your life has some blight or some inadequacy that you need to fix or fill results in an action that is contending, combative, and onerous for the person who is doing it. It's heavy. It's exhausting. So, it is not the action per se. It is not what we do; it is how we see. The fruit of our action is to cultivate an experience, a way of seeing. It's cultivating a perception.

So the reason for me giving fi sabeelallah is so that I experience that the world is not my enemy. I start getting real feedback that, in fact, my life works and that I don't have to worry about it. Things will work out.

One way of describing what we're busy with on this path (in addition to the things that we do like dhikr, salat, and sadaqa) is that we give. The real reward in the giving, the real purpose of doing this, is to change how you experience things or how you experience life. The real fruit of a well-lived life is not a vast accumulation of assets or feats of action. The real fruit of a successful life is a way of seeing. It's a way of viewing the world from a station of gratitude and fullness, and not a station of emptiness.

Allah SWT has put us amongst people, and he's made us human. And to make us human, we have to be damaged. This wild being that comes into the world as an infant needs to be civilised. It needs to be cauterised. It needs to have its passions restrained and constrained.

It needs to be taught to act conditionally. It needs to be taught to use language, to plan for the future, and to collaborate and cooperate. So, in a sense, we get reprogrammed to lose our original sense of fullness. Why? So that we can rediscover it. When we come into the world, we end up in a place of exile so that we can go home. And the going home is the recognition that it is all alright from the start.

This whole thing is miraculous and works by the most extraordinary design. This is one significance of the following description of the path: 'What is life but five prayers and waiting for death?'. This description of what it means to be a faqeer is not depressing or morbid. It is saying, 'My life is so full that I can die now. There's nothing else to be done other than to dance my dance of worship, which is the five prayers'. This is not life-negating but life-affirming. It's saying, 'It is all amazing, it is all extraordinary, it is all miraculous. There is nothing to be judged or fixed'.

There are two ways in which we try to manipulate the world to keep the world on our side. They're both toxic, but one is more toxic than the other. The first way is if we seek to ingratiate ourselves with the world. We want to be sweet with people; we want to manipulate people. The other is that we brutalise them, we beat them; we dominate or bully the other to get what we want.

Of the two, the most pernicious is the sweet thing - the idea that I can play little games of manipulation and stay in charge, to get from the world what I want. The first sign that I'm playing this game is that my attitude towards somebody changes instantly when they're no longer doing what I want them to do. 'Ah, you see now. You're not dancing to my tune. Now you're a bad person'. When you dominate people, it is obvious that you want to get something from them. When you manipulate people, however, there are two injuries. Not only are you trying to get something from them, but you are treating them like idiots in the process.

If we were full, there would be no restraint in our service. There would be no condition to our service. Our service would not deplete us. There would be no ill feeling about it. There would be no sense of being unjustly done by when we are called to serve. We would be a fullness that spontaneously empties.

May Allah SWT grant us nearness to Him,
May He grant us annihilation in Him,
May He grant us death before we die.

Chapter 3

WHICH OF THE BLESSINGS OF YOUR LORD ARE YOU GOING TO DENY?
Discourse 3: 7 November 2015

Bismillah ar-rahman ar-raheem

If seeing things as they are is not good enough for you, then you're not seeing things as they are. We mostly experience our lives as the successive replenishment of lack. Most of the inner traditions of the Orient have a view which is consistent with the Buddhist view that suffering is inevitable; that suffering or lack is the primary condition of human existence.

Because all things end. Everything that you pursue will, at some point, prove to be futile. But that futility can only be futile if the whole point is forward-looking. Because, clearly, looking forward, all things do come to an end. But what one forgets in the process of observing that things come to an end is that they were in the first place.

So how is it that we don't see that things are fixed? How is it that we experience things as broken? How is it that what we have is not enough and that we seek to take our lives elsewhere? In Surah Ar Rahman, Allah SWT keeps on repeating to us: which of His favours will we deny? We speak about the capacity to act unconditionally. But what we have to understand is that any truly unconditional act disavows an interest in the outcome. Otherwise, it's not unconditional. If you have an interest in the outcome, then, clearly, there's a condition that you're trying to manage. The moment that you act in order to produce an outcome, you are, by definition, saying to yourself that what you have isn't good enough.

The only reason why what you have isn't good enough is because you've given it a cursory examination. Many of you have attended the Personal Excellence programme that I teach, and you know that, during the programme, there's a day where we examine biographies. In this process, you arbitrarily put three or four people in a group who then each speak through the 33 events that have made them who they are.

What is amazing about those experiences is that, once somebody has gone through that account of their own life, the other people in that group can never see that person in the same way. They are always far more respectful and far more thoughtful towards the person who has spoken through their life in just an hour.

So the question is, why don't we generally respect people out there? Why does it have to take an hour through a biographic narrative for people to really get a sense of who you are and who they are? It is because we live life so much in the fast lane that we do not see things as they are. We don't take the time to recognize how things came to be where they are now.

And that's why they don't appear to be good enough. So, which of the blessings of your Lord are you going to deny? Well, you deny them partly because you don't recognize them in the first place - because you overlook them. How is it that we get ourselves into the miserable definitions of our lives where what we have is deemed inadequate, under threat, and flawed? It does such violence to the truth. We sit in a cornucopia of blessing and possibility, and the overriding register is the lack of rain.

We live in a country where the average South African citizen is actually quite a courteous person. All you have to do is go to a supermarket and see the courtesy of the lady at the till. Yet the overriding theme in our conversations with each other is a lament of crime, violence, and corruption. It is like we have a deeply vested interest in staying miserable.

And we repeat the story of the misery.

We must understand that our Rabb is our opinion of Him. He says so. He says, 'I am my slave's opinion of me'. If you have a poor opinion of your Rabb, He's going to show you a face which is going to be repulsive. If you have a good opinion of your Rabb, He's going to show you a face that is pleasant. How do you have a good opinion of your Rabb? You see what He has done as praiseworthy. And what has He done? He has done everything that's put the world in front of you, as it is right now.

In order to see just how praiseworthy it is, you actually have to give some attention to reflecting on how it got to be where it is now. And the more you examine how it got to be where it is now in the first place, the more you'll recognize that this is an extraordinary thing. It is like somebody talking through the 33 events of their biography. If you spend some time just allowing somebody the narrative time to explain how it is that they got here, you will see that they are amazing. It doesn't matter how much you dismissed the person prior to this for class reasons, for race reasons, or for ethnic reasons. Give that person the airtime to go through their account and, I guarantee you, you'll find something praiseworthy. You'll find something extraordinary. You'll find something worthy of affirmation.

So, which of the blessings of your Lord are you going to deny? Is your life not good enough here? Is what you've been given not an overflowing blessing, not a well of benevolence? Why is it that what you have is not good enough here? We had a discussion around cowardice. Cowardice is not having the courage to step outside of your own narrative of victimhood and to accept the full blessing of what your Rabb has put in front of you. Even if that blessing is death.

What a coward does is to hide away. A coward says, 'This world is dangerous. This world is not on my side. I need to protect myself from it'. That's cowardice. To make yourself available to your world or to be open to your world is courage. In fact, real strength is based on saying yes to life. And real weakness is based on having the snivelling narrative of victimhood, which allows you to get away with the idea that, somehow, you're being unjustly treated.

How can you be unjustly treated? How many incalculable blessings have to take place right now for you just to continue breathing? The real injustice would be that you never were. That is the real horror. The real horror is not oppression. The real horror is not that your life gets taken away from you. The real horror is if you never were in the first place. That the inky black vast emptiness of timeless space was not overcome to produce you.

That's the real possibility of horror. Anything that isn't that is, by definition, ecstatically praiseworthy.

Do you recognize that it might have been that you never were? And yet you are. It is a life even if you think it is difficult or compromised. And it doesn't matter if your life ends right now. What you've had prior to this is a life. None of that was owed to you.

May Allah SWT grant us nearness to Him,
May He grant us annihilation in Him,
May He grant us death before we die.

Chapter 4

YOUR LIFE IS A PRODUCT OF YOUR OPINION OF ALLAH SWT

Discourse 4: 19 August 2017

Bismillah ar-rahman ar-raheem

Allah SWT promises us that He is His slave's opinion of Him. That very simple phrase carries with it an almost terrifying responsibility and accountability. We know that wherever you turn in the face of Allah SWT. And whatever that face is saying to you, whatever expression that face has towards you, is a reflection of your opinion of the face. What comes first is the opinion. This means that, in the most deep and profound sense, the world that we deal with is our product. What we experience from the world is our own creation. The way in which we experience the world - how we experience the world's engagement with us and other people's engagement with us - is absolutely and singularly our own accountability.

This is a lesson that people in this age swallow very hard at. It is so easy for us to make the woes of our life the fault of some other. 'I've been oppressed, therefore I am poor, and the world is miserable.' 'The city that I live in is violent and therefore I'm unsafe.' 'People around me are self-serving and therefore I have to control them.' 'My life is difficult, my life has problems, and I am needy of other people's intervention in my interest. Otherwise, my life is a disaster.'

All of these experiences of the world, which are challenging and injurious to us and which makes us feel like we're victims of the world, are our own creation. What comes first is not the world's behaviour towards you. What comes first is your opinion of the world. No matter how justified you think your ill feeling is, no matter how correct you think you are in believing that you're being treated like a victim and being treated unfairly, no matter how just your outrage is – understand that the thing that you're outraged at is your product. You have made it. Because He has said - and He doesn't lie - that He is His slave's opinion of Him.

So if you have a bad experience of His face, it is your opinion of your Rabb that has produced that face. And if you're miserable and you seek to change your experience of the world, then don't seek to go and get more from the world or demand that the world treats you better. Change your opinion of the world. Change your opinion of your Rabb. Learn, wherever you see a curse, to find the blessing. Make it your habit to find the blessing.

So, the man has lost his foot in an accident. He could spend the rest of his life wailing about the fact that he has a missing foot. He could also say, 'Well, what's the benefit that has come out of this?'. And if he thought about it carefully he'd say, 'Well, at least I have another foot. I can still walk, I've got a leg. I've experienced such kindness from other people, who have rallied around me and helped and supported me in my crisis'. If he looked for it, he could find at least as many, if not more, blessings to the injury that he's had than curses.

Understand that if you take whatever He gives you - whatever His face provides you with - if you take that and you choose to find a blessing in it, then what will come subsequently will be a blessing. But if He presents you with something and you choose to find in it a curse, then He will visit you with more curses. And how do we know this?

Because Allah SWT has given us other human beings as the practice ground or as the kindergarten to understand how the rules of intent work. He says all our actions are judged by their intention. All our actions are judged by Him by their intention. Also, our actions are judged by other people based on their intention.

How often have you heard someone say 'Such-and-such behaved so badly. But don't worry, his intentions were good' and that forgives the behaviour? We ourselves judge people by their intention. We know that if you are kind to somebody and he responds in an ungrateful way, then you will never give that person anything again. If you give somebody some food or some help and he treats you like it was owed to him - like it was his right over you to get it - the next time that person asks for anything you're going to say, 'I'm not giving him anything. He's ungrateful.'

That person's ingratitude disables your generosity.

If, however, you do the slightest thing for the person and you get a sense of genuine gratitude out of the person, then the next time it's easier to give to that person. So Allah SWT gives us our interactions with other people as the practice ground where we can learn how He deals with us.

In any moment where you haven't died, there's more blessing than curse, by definition. So, in any given situation, if you are still alive one moment to the next, there's an impossible, incalculable number of things that have gone right without your managing the affair that have allowed you to carry on and stay alive. Which means that not to look at any situation that's in front of you with deep gratitude is not seeing the truth of the matter. When you see what's in front of you with deep gratitude and you truly say alhumdullilah, it is like a human being that you give something to saying thank you. It's easier to give to that person.

So your good opinion of your Rabb is translated into an ongoing recitation of gratitude towards your Rabb. And if you make it your habit to respond to what your Rabb gives you with gratitude and thankfulness, then the face that He will start to show you will be a pleasing face. A bad opinion is one that is rooted in resentment. Resentment says, 'I haven't been given enough'. A good opinion is based on gratitude. Gratitude says, 'I've been given in excess of my due'.

Any human being who consistently reminds themselves of how profoundly they've been given in excess of their due will solicit the most copious and unrestrained gifts from their Rabb. And those gifts will not just be gifts of material things. Those gifts will be the gifts that matter. Those gifts will be the gift of a peaceful heart, of certitude, of a deep knowing that your life is not arbitrary, and you aren't being batted around by forces beyond your control. It will be knowing that you're in the middle of a world that has your best interests at heart, because the world that you're in is His face. You don't have to look after yourself. You're already looked after in ways that you can't even begin to fathom.

So the most useful work that we can do starts with taking responsibility for what it feels like to be ourselves. And when we find in ourselves any traces of resentment or ill feeling, we must immediately go to work to change the character of that resentment or ill feeling to one that's rooted in gratitude. Because that is learning the habit of having a good opinion of your Rabb. It is that opinion that produces the world.

The kuffaar have the opinion that we are material objects being driven by forces beyond our control; things like natural selection and survival of the fittest are mechanical programmes that produce our lives. This is just so false. You are not the product of the world. Your world is your product because your world is the face that your Rabb gives you based on your opinion of Him.

If your world is not satisfying to you, then stop trying to fix the world and abuse it. Change your opinion of Him and change your opinion of His world, and your world will change. I can say this on personal authority. I don't think I'm different from any other human being of this age. I've also had my fair share of victimhood in my life. I've also had my fair share of being done in, of being ill-treated, and of being done injustice too. And I can say with the benefit of hindsight that all the suffering I had on the basis of this experience, of being done in, was my own product. I produced it. It's a great sadness that you have to bump into this truth when you're 58. Hopefully, if you discover it when you're younger, you can rescue a little bit more of your life.

May Allah SWT grant us nearness to Him,
May He grant us annihilation in Him,
May Allah SWT grant shifa to all of the people of our circle who are ill.

Chapter 5

TAKE FROM YOUR LIFE FOR YOUR DEATH
Discourse 5: 25 March 2019

Bismillah ar-rahman ar-raheem

Rasullulah (s.a.w.s.) is reported to have advised us that we should take from our lives for our death, and from our death for our lives.

Let's first examine what it means to take from your life for your death.

One can imagine that the end of a matter is also the purpose of the matter, and the purpose of the matter is also the zenith - its highest point. This means we have to conclude that, since the end of our life is death, it has to mean, in a sense, that the purpose of our life is to have a good death. The zenith of our life, the pinnacle of our life, is a good death. It implies that our whole life is, in a sense, a practice ground for that final examination. It is a gymnasium to develop a particular skill which will eventually be tested.

And what is this skill? This skill is being able to hand over unconditionally, without reserve, and absolutely the whole matter to Allah SWT in an instant. When we die, we don't get anything. When we die, we give everything. We give everything completely and unconditionally. Well, it either gets given unconditionally, or it gets taken away from us unconditionally.

The only choice we have is the intention by which we engage in the moment. The fact that everything is going to go is foregone. It is a fact like an ox. That is how things are.

So, how do we live our lives in such a way that, in living our lives, we prepare for our deaths? What do we need to do to make that possible?

Every moment that we face is, in a sense, like a T-junction. Every moment that we face puts us on the horns of a dilemma. Basically, it says,

'What do you want from this situation that you're in and what does Allah SWT want from you? What do you want to get, and what should you be giving?'.

This is a moment-by-moment challenge. That challenge never goes away. Every moment that you are alive faces you with that distinction. What does He want from you and what do you want?

When you act on the basis of what you want, you get stuck. When you act on the basis of what you want, you don't learn the propensity to give away unconditionally. Which means you don't exercise the muscle that you need in order to face your death. Taking from your life for your death means that you use every moment that you are alive as an opportunity to respond to what Allah SWT has put in front of you in that situation.

One has to be at pains to point out that, very often, what He puts in front of you doesn't suit your culturally defined conventions of good behaviour. In fact, acting on the basis of our culturally defined conventions of good behaviour is not a way of changing, it is not a way of giving up. It is a way of staying the same. It is a way of ossifying. Getting stuck. Stagnating.

So the distressing thing about this is that there is no formula. It is about learning to hear what He whispers to you in your heart and responding to that whispering, even if it looks contradictory to what the authorities may be telling you at the time. In a sense, it is only the person who is truly spontaneous – who can, in a moment, in a flash, give up everything – who is able to die and is able to die well.

So, if we say that every moment we are alive faces us with a T-junction, then the left of that T-junction is what you want, and the right is when you ask yourself, 'What does He want?'. Don't think that this is just about being a goody two-shoes. Sometimes, the right-hand turn is about challenging your community, it is about challenging the too easily brokered conventions of good behaviour that get us stuck.

If you look at our tradition, very often people of tasawwuf are considered to be quite eccentric and a little bit unhinged. This is precisely because of this reason. Is this not the implication of the engagement between Nabi Musa and Khidr? Three times Khidr did things that Nabi Musa found completely irrational. Things that completely defied Nabi Musa's sense of good behaviour. Khidr represents to us the kind of consciousness that we are trying to occupy, which is to do what is right, even if it flies into the face of convention.

Being able to forgo everything is a fundamentally wild way of being. It is a fundamentally natural way of being, like a thunderstorm or a tidal wave. This is not an ordinary tame human being as we know it. So that's what it means to take from your life for your death. To take from your life for your death is to learn how to forego, to learn to transcend, to learn not to be trapped by convention, and to learn to constantly challenge your need for affirmation from the world and your need from the world.

We know that he who wants something from the other is the other's slave. If I want something from you, your ability to withhold it from me gives you power over me. However, we are not aimed at an event of enslavement. We are aimed at an event of stellar, ecstatic, and stupendous transcendence. Its name is death.

That's the great explosion, it's the great catapulting beyond. Make yourself worthy of that event. Make it easy for you to engage in that event by learning how to catapult yourself out of the constraints of convention and your petty needs and concerns, beyond the good opinion of others and the possessions that you want to have. That's what it means to take from your life for your death.

We also have the opposite, taking from your death for your life. There are a number of significances in this. In the first instance, taking from your death for your life means that you learn to see things in perspective. 'Oh, it's calamitous, I spoiled the cake with rotten eggs'. 'Oh, it is a disaster, my car is broken'. 'Oh, it is a calamity, they have broken into my house and stolen the TV'. Actually, there is only one calamity, and that calamity is that you are going to die. When you constantly remind yourself of the proximity and reality of your death, it puts all these other calamities into perspective.

The fact of the matter is that we consistently sweat the small stuff. We consistently make what is insignificant, significant. As a result, we turn our life into a misery that it really shouldn't be and needn't be.

The second attribute of the skill of taking from your death for your life is that it enables courage; it enables an ability to forgo. You realise that there is nothing to be preserved, that there is nothing to hold on to. You realise that all of your possessions are going to go. All your accumulations have to go. They will go. They can either go in one fell swoop or they can go incrementally. But go they will.

Everything that you own will be owned by somebody else very soon. Sooner than you realise. It is always sooner than you realise. Which means that, if you are aware of your death and you remind yourself of your death, it doesn't only release you from regret, but also from clinging.

Remembering death is also a good cure for fearing what you may lose. How do you manipulate somebody who is willing to die, who is quite capable of dying immediately? How do you force that person to do what you want them to do? The only person who is truly free is the person who can die in an instant.

Sometimes, we think people like that are necessarily suicidal, necessarily morbid. But that isn't the case at all. In fact, it is only the person who is quite comfortable with the possibility of losing everything who is truly living a life. You have to understand that if you cannot lose the thing, you don't have it. It has you.

There is a marvellous story of this pirate ship that was going down, and some of the pirates were in a lifeboat and some of them were in the sea. One of the pirates had jumped into the sea from a sinking ship with his gold. As he was going down, his friends yelled to him to drop the gold. 'For heaven's sake, drop the gold and we can save you'. But the man couldn't drop the gold, so the gold pulled him down and he drowned.

The remaining pirates on the lifeboat were all very morose, thinking about their poor comrade who was lost. After a while, one of the pirates said, 'It was really sad. He really had to have his gold". And then another one said, 'No, that's not right. It was not him that had the gold. It was the gold that had him'.

You're the slave of what you can't lose. Become comfortable with the possibility of irrevocable loss, and you are free. The only truth which makes it possible for you to become comfortable with irrevocable loss is to be aware of the proximity of your death. If you have seen somebody die of an ailment or an accident, you realise just how fleeting this life is. How frail it is. How incredibly delicate it is. How quickly it can get snuffed out. It is not a solid thing at all. It is a snap of a finger, and it is gone.

Shaykh Abdul Qadir often said, 'We are in a rush to death.' We're on this breathtaking rollercoaster of life, plummeting towards this finality. The person who knows that has a life. The person who can lose their life has a life. The person who cannot lose their life doesn't have a life. They have servitude.

May Allah SWT grant us nearness to Him,
May Allah SWT grant us annihilation in Him,
May Allah SWT grant us death before we die.

Chapter 6

DEATH AS YOUR ADVISOR
Discourse 6: 9 March 2013

Bismillah ar-rahman ar-raheem

The remembrance of death is one of the many devices on our path that we use in order to clarify our intent. The remembrance of death helps to clarify and polish our hearts, so that we can experience the proximity of the Rabb.

By definition, for the living, the proximity of death will always be a reasonably speculative idea because, if you aren't dead, then you are speculating about being dead. If we view it from that point of view, then it's very important to regard the proximity of your death with great gravity. It is far too easy to make this matter a speculative matter. I often find that when I ask someone, 'Do you think you can die now?', the person says, 'Yes'. Alhumdullilah, that's impressive. But sometimes the response comes too quickly. You are almost tempted to ask the person, 'Really? Do you really think you can die? Now?'.

So one must be aware that, when you are reminding yourself of the proximity of your death, it doesn't happen in an offhand or cursory way, but with great gravity. The most useful times to learn how to use this device is when you've had a near miss because then it's somehow less speculative. When you've almost fallen off the motorcycle; when you were one step away from stepping off the edge of the building; when you stood near the snake and it struck and got your trousers.

When these events happen, the near misses, that is your Rabb's great generosity to you. Not because he saved your life, but because he took you to the edge so you could look down the abyss and talk about or consider or reflect on the proximity of your death with some real gravity, with some realness. Then the device becomes truly powerful because you've smelt it; you've smelt death. It's not speculative anymore. It has a real force to it.

So why is it that we should do this? Other people would consider it a morbid thing to do. Well, if you want to succeed at the play, you rehearse. And if we consider that the final examination that we're going to write is the grave, then maybe we should afford ourselves the opportunity to rehearse for the event.

So, in the first instance, it's about taking from your life for your death. It's about dedicating a portion of your life to rehearse giving up. All the practices of our deen are rehearsals for giving up. Your salat is a rehearsal for giving up, for submission, for becoming defenceless. Your sawm is the same. Going to sleep is the same. Because the Rasul (s.a.w.s.) has reminded us that sleep is like death. In both, you get overwhelmed by unconsciousness; you disappear into unconsciousness.

There are lots of periods in our lives that are rehearsals for dying. This is a very useful rehearsal to do because your death is the most predictable thing about you. If you fail at the event – not that anybody fails at dying, but they fail at the proper engagement of death – then the horror of that engagement is an eternal horror. Because, when you die, there isn't a moment behind that. Which means that if you take terror at the loss of everything into that moment, then that terror will last forever.

So our insight here is that the fire is not a metaphor, it is a reality. It is the reality faced by the one who cannot lose everything unconditionally and is asked to do so. That horror of having everything ripped out of your hands, that your entire life is negated, doesn't have a second rehearsal to this. It's done. It's finished. So that horror lasts forever.

That moment can also be a moment of delight if you've practised submitting. This is not just in terms of making all the right noises in Arabic, but it's when you've done your salat and you've given in – really given in. When your neighbours come to you with a problem, you help the neighbour. When the lady was being assaulted, you intervened in her interest. You put yourself at the service of your Rabb. You gave over what your Rabb asked of you. Then, when He finally comes for the big prize – the great handing over – it is easy. And then, that delight of joyfully handing over unconditionally to your Rabb is also forever.

So the rehearsal of death is taking from your life for your death. The Rasul (s.a.w.s.) said that you must take from your life for your death. But he also said that you must take from your death for your life. In other words, this rehearsal of your death is somehow extraordinarily empowering. Because when you rehearse your death, you realize how many of the things that you perceive and make important to yourself are frivolous and of no import. They are silly.

In the face of what really matters, is it really an issue what colour the car is? Or that somebody threw a stone through your window? What becomes apparent when you look at the proximity of death, is that it demands of you to strip away the inessential and to focus on what your Rabb wants from you, here and now. So, in that way, your death enables your life. Because it means you stop wasting your energy in frivolous activities that are just going to bleed your life energy into all the wrong channels.

Every one of us has come into this world with a charge from our Rabb; a charge which is of such gravity that the entire universe depends on it. And how can we say that? Because every human alive is epicentral to existence. Where is the rest of the universe in regard to you? Surely, it's in every direction, pointing away into infinity. So who's in the middle? You're in the middle. Who's the point of the universe that you're in? You're the point of the universe that you're in. You are here for an extraordinarily significant purpose.

It might not be extraordinarily significant in the eyes of other people, but they're irrelevant in terms of the view of Allah SWT. He has made you the keystone, the one element that is crucially necessary for this drama to unfold with the highest degree of beauty and eloquence that it can. Are you going to rise to the occasion? Or are you going to waste your life energy in frivolous and inessential pursuits?

What you find, when you do what your Rabb has called you into existence to do, is that He allies the whole of existence behind you. All the help that you need will be given to you. But if you waste the opportunity because your head was so busy with all sorts of things that you can't even work out what the priorities are, you'll find that the whole universe will find you ugly and objectionable and will resist you. And the experience of that resistance is that we then get depressed, and we have a sense of powerlessness and a sense of meaninglessness in our day-to-day lives.

So, the device of using our death as an advisor has two benefits. It has the benefit of taking from your life for your death because there's nothing like studying for the final exam. There's nothing like reciting to yourself the propensity to lose unconditionally so that, when you are asked to do that, you do it eloquently with no arguments. Secondly, when you use your death for your life, it helps to clear the priorities. Your Rabb says to you, 'Now that you've had the near miss and the bullet has grazed the bridge of your nose, what are you going to do with the rest of the days left to you? Because you never know when the next bullet is going to come'.

Alhumdullilah.

May Allah SWT grant us nearness to Him,
May Allah SWT grant us annihilation in Him,
May Allah SWT grant us death before we die.

Chapter 7

THE FULLNESS OF TIME
Discourse 7: 28 June 2014

Bismillah ar-rahman ar-raheem

Imam Kamardine has just reminded us from Allah SWT that all human endeavour is futile. In the face of time, all humans are lost, and all human affairs are futile. One likes to think of that as a big-picture announcement: in the fullness of time, when the last day comes, whatever you would have done will all be swept away. That is true.

But this is not only true in a big picture sense. What this is saying is that anything that is done with the hope of achieving an outcome is fundamentally futile. All human endeavour is concerned with outcomes – well, at least the bulk of human endeavour as we know it. In fact, the very word 'intention' is a future-facing, outward-directed word. 'I intend to do this' implies that I have a goal.

It is true to say that, in the fullness of time, the goal that you are pursuing - even if you should get it - will be swept away by the winds and the sands of time. No matter how significant you are, no matter how dramatic the achievement. There will be a point where not even the most well-known names in history will be remembered. They will be gone.

Consider how short the period of time that we've been on the planet is. In the time that we've been on the planet, the myriad of names, except that of Hazrat Adam, have all appeared in the last ten thousand years. Even the most memorable ones. What about the many generations that went before that? They have been swept away; their wishes, their endeavours, and their concerns are no longer there.

So it is true to say that, in the fullness of time, all that you aspire to achieve will be swept away. But this futility that is the product of future-directed behaviour, the product of our intention, isn't just that in the fullness of time whatever you're going to do is going to be swept away. The futility is actually inside the structure of intention.

You see, if I do this in order to get that, the assumption is that getting that is going to make me happy. And therein lies the problem. Because the same miserable person that started the activity, that started the commencement part of the journey towards the realization of intent, ends up at the outcome.

So, the man is disgruntled with his wife and he thinks he needs to leave her. So he leaves her. He marries a new woman, and within six months, he's got the same problem. And he blames the wife, not realizing that the same miserable man that left the previous marriage went into the new one.

This is true for all outcome-directed intentions, particularly if you think that getting what you want is going to make you happy. 'I am poor, and I need money to be happy.' So I work really hard and get lots of money, only to discover that I am the same discontented wretch, but only now I'm a rich one. 'I am fat and I want to get thin.' I go through all this starvation and suffering to become thin, and it's the same miserable man who is now a thin man.

Whatever it is that you pursue that you think has happiness on the other side of the rainbow is a mirage. The end of the rainbow just moves away when you get to where you thought it was. You never get to the pot of gold at the end of the rainbow. However, you construct your intent, as soon as there is a future to that intent, it is futile. The same miserable person ends up on the other side of the activity that is going to produce the imagined happiness.

That isn't to say that you won't be happy temporarily. You may well be. You worked very hard and bought a brand-new car. The first two days are magnificent. You smell the wonderful smell of the new car. It's comfortable and delightful to drive. And then, on the third day, somebody upsets you and you overlook the pleasure of the new car. You become habituated to the pleasure of the new car, and it suddenly is not quite so satisfying. Now you want two new cars. So this futility that human intention delivers us in is not just the fact that outcomes are, by definition, futile because they are going to be swept away by the sands of time. The futility is inside the very structure of future-directed intention. It is the equivalent of drinking salt water for thirst.

illal ladhina aamanu
Except those who believe

Who are those who believe? Those who believe are those who know that Allah SWT is the best of providers, that Allah SWT is also the best of planners. That it's not up to you to define outcomes; they belong to Him. You trust because that is what imaan surely means: faith. You trust that the outcome will be okay. You don't act out of the need for an outcome.

That almost means nonsense with the idea of intention. Why do you act? Why act if there is no outcome? I don't need to act for an outcome because I know that all outcomes delivered to me have been spectacular and better than what I would have planned.

And isn't this true? Look back on your life. Can you truly claim that what you've received is all due to your ingenuity? If you do, this would be the most outrageous assertion of ingratitude. If you look back at your life, you'll recognize in an instant that your life is a product of something far bigger than your own intelligence. That should fill the heart with gratitude.

Without gratitude, imaan is meaningless. You cannot have faith if you don't have gratitude. How can you look at the future and say, 'I believe that the outcomes will be okay' if you haven't fully appraised the past and you haven't recognized the overwhelming mercy and beneficence of your Lord in the past.

So, it is an easy sentence:

illal ladhina aamanu
Except those who believe

but it has a thick book's worth of implications.

Those who look into the future to be happy are busy with a futile endeavour because that just affirms their emptiness. Those who believe are those who look at their past and realize that their lives are miraculous. They don't have to govern outcomes because outcomes are going to be stupendous. All they have to do is aml as-salihaat. They have to do what their Rabb wants from them.

You don't have to come up with a plan. He's the genius. He will show you the plan. You just do the right thing, here and now. There's a captain in charge of the ship. You don't have to go and take over. Subhanallah. He's in charge. The right action is a spontaneous overflowing of gratitude for having received in excess of your due in the past. It is not an action aimed at manipulating a better future. Good action is based on gratitude. Gratitude is not going somewhere. It has come from somewhere.

Actions based on gratitude have the opposite structure to how we generally view intent. One way of looking at intention is basically 'I haven't got this, so I'm going to do this to get that' or 'I do this in order to get that'. This means that I'm doing something to get something I don't have. It is a neediness or an emptiness that I want to fill.

What if you make the assertion that I've got more than I deserve? Do you not act? Of course, you act. But the structure of how your intention operates is the opposite. It's almost as if the word intention struggles with that reality because it's not like there is anything that you want to get. Instead, you think, 'I've got so much that I don't know what to do with it. I want to give it away'. My intent is not an emptiness that seeks to be filled. It is a fullness which empties.

I experience the overflowingness of my Rabb. I'm a fullness that empties. If my action is based on a fullness that empties, then every single transaction is given to give away. That's freedom. I'm not doing this so that you think I'm important. I'm not doing this so that you like me. I'm not doing this as an investment in our relationship. I'm doing this because it occurs to me that my Rabb wants me to do this for you right now. Unconditionally.

Bismillah. Bismillah. What else could the word Bismillah mean? If you're saying 'In the name of Allah' are you saying that you're dedicating it to Him? No, you're saying, 'This is Your work; this is not mine'.

Bismillah. Bismillah ar-rahman ar-raheem. This is a celebration of Your name, the One who withholds catastrophe and the One who grants favour. The merciful. The beneficent. The One who will look after you.

So, take those first three assertions of Surat al As'r:

wa-l-'asr
innal insaana la-fi khusr
By time, man is completely at a loss.

Time makes his endeavours futile, both in terms of their outcome, but also in terms of the very thing that they're trying to achieve.

illaladhina aamanuu

Except those who have full hearts and therefore trust their Lord.

And they no longer have a future; they have forgone the future. They've handed the future to Him because they know that the past has been extraordinary, so why won't the future be?

wa-'amil-us-saalihati

And act accordingly

wa tawasaw bil-haqqi

And those who encourage each other towards truth.

And what is the truth? The truth is that there is a guardian Lord in charge, you aren't the master of outcomes, and that you're far happier if you forgo outcomes and leave it in His hands. In other words, not only do you have to believe, but you remind other people as well. Because that is what you do when you're calling them to the truth: 'Just relax. Don't get yourself into such a tizzy. What are you getting so freaked out about? You know, if the bullet that has your name on it is going to hit you, there's absolutely nothing you're going to do to avoid it. That thing was already loaded in the rifle before endless time'. Subhanallah.

And so, we encourage each other to the reality that there is a guardian Lord in charge, and we don't have to be in charge.

wa tawasaw bi-s-sabr

And we encourage each other to patience.

Surely, patience is the same thing as aml as-salihaat because aml as-salihaat means that I don't act based on what I want to get. I'm patient with that. I know that my Rabb will look after that. I will act on the basis of what He wants from me.

So I'm forbearing with what I want from life because I know it will be good. I know it will be better. I do what He wants from me. Not only do I do it, but I encourage you to do the same. And why do I encourage you to do the same? It's because I want you to be happy. Because I know that when I act on the basis of the conviction that what my Rabb has given me is extraordinary and I don't have to worry about the outcome, I'm deeply happy. And the times when I forget - as we do - I'm deeply miserable. It's a really unpleasant way to be. So, because you're my brother and because I have concern for you and I do not want to see you suffer, I tell you, 'Listen, if you don't want to suffer, then remember the truth. The truth is that He is in charge. Look back at your life. Wasn't it magnificent? And therefore, do what He wants you to do. Stop acting on the basis of what you want. Be patient with what you want'.

Alhumdullilah. All of these point to the commitment that we should have on this path, which is to make the principal endeavour of our day-to-day life the clarification of our intent. That's the core endeavour. That's the key thing that we're accountable for, that our life is constructed against. This clarification of intent is the first flight of stairs on the path.

So, when Allah SWT says:

wa-l-'asr
innal insaana la-fi khusr

it does not mean that you don't work.

If you make the purpose of your work the thing that you're trying to achieve in this world, it's futile. How about making the purpose to clarify what is happening behind your eyes? It's still working. But the purpose of the work is in the inner, it's not in the outer.

There's nothing wrong with work. You've got to struggle. How do you propose to actually crack the code of forgoing if you don't do things? But you've got to make the purpose of this the project working on yourself, rather than trying to achieve things in the world. If you make the purpose of the day-to-day endeavour the clarification of your intent, you can only succeed. Because that is deliberately cultivating imaan. If you make achieving outcomes the purpose of your day-to-day endeavour, then take it from Him.

He said it in one very simple sentence:

wa-l-'asr
innal insaana la-fi khusr

You are busy with something futile. You're drinking salt water for thirst.

May our Rabb grant us nearness to Him,
May He grant us annihilation in Him,
May He grant us death before we die.

Chapter 8

THE PRESENT
RESPONSIBILITY
Discourse 8: 23 February 2019

Bismillah ar-rahman ar-raheem

Sidi Yusuf Abdur-Rahman said something very profound in the week that has stayed with me. I think it's very useful. He had been asked about destiny and how destiny is also reflected in one's own behaviour. If I misbehave, am I predestined to misbehave? I may do violence to his explanation, but I'm going to try to repeat more or less what he said because I think it's very helpful.

Before I describe his account of this, I need to make a point about how we experience things and how we experience time. We have a certain way of thinking about time. This creates the conditions that things appear to us in a certain way, which might be doing violence to the truth or at least creating some inaccuracy.

Our experience is that there's this long past that has gone before us. Then we have now, the moment that we're in. Then we imagine a long future, and we see the moment that we're in as a tiny blip, a small thing – in fact, a minuscule thing – in the face of the weight of everything that's gone before, and the weight of everything that's going to happen subsequently.

That way of looking at time is really a construct in our minds. There's another way of looking at time, which is that you're only ever in now. You aren't in now yesterday and you aren't in now tomorrow. You're only ever in now, now. This suggests that the moment you're in is all that there is. It's like a theatre that things can come into and leave. In other words, the big thing is the theatre – that's what exists. Not this imagined series of events that have happened before. They're gone. The present – the moment – is a vessel that has things fed into it, that has things removed from it. And all that ever is, is the vessel. Those things that are removed from it are as if they have never been. Because they're gone. And those things that are yet to come are also as if they aren't going to be. Because they haven't happened. So all that there is, is what's in this vessel. This moment is not a small dot in parentheses between the long past and the long future. In fact, the big thing is the moment. The past and the future are little illusions tacked on at either end.

Now, when you have this view of time, what Sidi Yusuf said becomes significant. He said you no longer have volition over everything that's happened before. It has departed from you. It has become part of the mass of things that have happened that have produced who you are now. In other words, even your own misbehaviour in the past, once it has become past, is no longer with you. It has become part of what has produced you. This means that the totality of the past, which includes your behaviour, is by decree. By decree means it is outside of your volition. You cannot change it. He points out that while you cannot change what has happened, including your own misbehaviour, you do have the responsibility to deal appropriately with the moment that you're in.

All the things that have happened before now have configured the theatre that you're looking at. How you respond to what is in the theatre in front of you is up to you. This suggests a way to understand the term responsibility. He says responsibility is really two words: response-ablity or your ability to respond. It is how you respond to the totality of what's in front of you now. Which means, you have no volition over what has happened. It is a fact like an ox; it is indisputable. And all of that – the totality of it – is from Allah SWT. The only thing that matters is the theatre that you're facing – the moment that you're in – and how you respond to the moment that you're in. That's all that matters.

The view of running a past much like running an account can get one into trouble. If you do that, you view your past as having this immense momentum that produces who you are now. 'I've been made like this. I'm this kind of person. I'm that kind of person. I've been ill-treated in the past and, because I've been ill-treated in the past, my life has been damaged, and that's why I cannot respond appropriately in the moment that I'm in. I've been done in, in some way. I cannot be courteous to somebody who is less privileged than me because I've been brought up in a life of privilege.' So I view my past as having a momentum to it that produces my response now. That's not true. You always have absolute autonomy with regard to your response now.

So, irrespective of what's happened before – view that as part of the props on the stage, without any ill feeling and without any rancour – consider what your response is to this stage. What is the most noble response you can have to the props, as they have been put on the stage now? The nobility of your response is something you have complete volition over. That response gets fed as part of the detritus that goes into the past.

The further thing to this, of course, is that nothing that has happened to you exists outside the significance you have granted it. The significance of what it is does not exist independently of what you designate as significant.

I'll give you an example. There was a point in my life when I was a conscript to the South African army in the days of the apartheid, and I really didn't want to go. I had very serious ideological problems with going to the army and so it was catastrophic that I got caught and I ended up in a situation where I couldn't evade it. I had to go. At that time, it was one of the worst things that could have conceivably happened to me. My life had collapsed. With the benefit of hindsight, however, I learned so much in those two years of my national service that I recognize it now as one of the most formative periods of my life. In fact, it was a very good experience, a very constructive experience, a very maturing experience. So, when I was close to the event, it was a catastrophe. The significance of it to me was catastrophic. And now that I have some maturity, the significance of the thing is a blessing. So what was it, was it a catastrophe or was it a blessing? Actually, that's irrelevant. What is relevant is what I've designated it to be. What I designate the thing to be is always now, in the present.

In that sense, the past really doesn't define us at all. We define the past. Because we designate the significance of the past. So, this is true even with our own misbehaviour, which has now become part of the total canvas that is the backdrop to your being – the preceding backdrop to your being. You can choose to see your own misbehaviour as a blessing. You can say,

'Ah, you see, if I hadn't done that, I wouldn't have learnt this or that'. That doesn't mean you give yourself license to continue misbehaving. But it means that it gives you the right not to be defined by your past, but to define your past.

So, once it's in the past, everything is perfectly predestined – you cannot alter it. But you can certainly alter your response in the moment that you're in.

We also know that nothing changes the decree except the du'a of a Muslim, of a believer. This is again one of those things that one can get very pious about, but what does it actually mean? Du'a means that you deeply know that nothing is as it seems; that Allah SWT can bring forth the angel or the bird from the rock. He can bring forth life from the dead. He can make all things happen. This means that you are affirming that when you look at your Rabb in a spirit of gratitude and trust, He will transform that which seems inevitable. This moment that you're in and what's manifesting in the moment that you're in is not cast in stone. It is not decreed. Because it is in this magical space of the theatre of now, where creation happens continuously and creation, by definition, is ever-new. Allah SWT recreates the whole story, moment by moment by moment. And, because He recreates it, He creates it afresh. He creates it anew.

So, you aren't stuck in a straitjacket of this inevitability, of this locomotive of the past that's driving you forward. Because every moment has this miraculous propensity to be ever fresh, to be ever new, to be a completely changed situation. Radically changed. So, if you view yourself as this product of a series of events that have an inevitability to them then, yes, you have turned yourself into a victim of those events. And you have therefore said that everything is by His decree. But you don't realize that His decree is something that you participate in, in the moment that you're in. His decree isn't something that had happened in the past. His decree happens now. You have an interactive, intelligent relationship with what He is doing now. You're His dance partner. You help to galvanise and to create the decree – to produce the decree.

He has made it such that all things that have happened prior to now have only happened in order to make you possible. And He's done that for no other reason than for you to be stupendously enthralled with Him, amazed with Him, enchanted with Him, in love with Him. That's why all that has happened prior to now has happened.

But, for that to happen, you must occupy your space as being His friend. That's what the word 'wali' means: His friend. His companion. The One that you're companionable with. The One that you are conspiratorial with. The One you sit with one evening and have a conversation with. He is intimate. He is close. Otherwise, why does He say He is closer to you than your jugular vein? He is not removed.

From one point of view, there's no other: He is you and you are He. And so, in this companionability that you can establish in the moment – now – with Him, you produce the possibility of you truly helping to create the world that you're in. And that completely transcends this idea of you being this blind object that's just been spat out, by decree, at the end of a historical chain of events.

May Allah SWT grant us nearness to Him.
May Allah SWT grant us annihilation in Him.
May Allah SWT grant us death before we die.

Chapter 9

WHY DO WE SUFFER?
Discourse 9: 26 September 2015

Bismillah ar-rahman ar-raheem

I've had two conversations today where the theme of suffering was at issue, both of which implied the question: 'Why do we suffer?'. We claim that Allah SWT is a benevolent Rabb, so why do we, as individuals, suffer? Why is there suffering in the world and why do human beings suffer? This is clearly quite a weighty matter that goes right to the core of being human. In my experience, it doesn't matter how privileged people are. If you scratch a human being, you find suffering. Under the surface, every human being suffers.

I'd like to preface what I'm going to say today with a caution that this examination is exploratory. I do not intend it to demean somebody's suffering. I do not intend it to be an exhaustive examination of the issue. The issue of suffering is as broad as humanity itself, and it is not amenable to a twenty-minute dars. But I'll try.

The first thing you've got to understand about suffering is that it has got nothing to do with somebody's social status or station in the world. We get indoctrinated into the view that the privileged don't suffer, and the underprivileged and the poor suffer. In my experience, this just isn't true.

There's no correlation between how rich you are and the degree to which you suffer. The privileged don't have a monopoly on happiness, and the underprivileged don't have a monopoly on suffering. In fact, there's very little relationship between your socioeconomic status and the degree to which you suffer. The further thing one must remember about suffering is that, in essence, all suffering is based on an illusion. Because, as long as I'm alive, it goes well with me.

When somebody suffers, there is a bit of an accusation. They're saying, 'The world's being mean to me. I'm suffering'. This accusation must be false. There are so many things that are beyond what you can manage that have to go right for you to be able to take the next breath, that it cannot be true that you have somehow been done in. In so far as you are alive, there's always more privilege and blessing in your life than dysfunction and brokenness. If we define our lives to be cast in suffering, we are asserting a demonstrable falsehood. It cannot be the truth.

So many things have to go well even for a quadriplegic person to be able to take the next breath. To stay alive, so many things have to go well spontaneously that, in so far as that person is alive, it goes well with him. If it ceases to go well with you, then you're dead. The appropriate way to respond to the insight that it goes well with me is not an accusation of suffering, but a declaration of gratitude.

This doesn't mean that one doesn't suffer. Just because suffering is illusory, it does not mean that the experience of suffering isn't real. That is like laughing at a man who gets a fright from a rubber snake because he's getting a fright from an illusion. Well, the snake is an illusion. However, there is nothing illusory about the fear; there is nothing illusory about the inner experience. Similarly, there's nothing illusory about the experience of suffering. We certainly do experience it, but the experience is based on a misapprehension of the truth.

All suffering expresses two kinds of vulnerability. The first is, 'I am vulnerable because I have not been granted enough,' and the second is, 'I am vulnerable because I am under threat'. The first element of suffering is to look back at your past and to say that you've somehow been short-changed. The second is to look forward to the future with a sense of anxiety and distrust. Shaykh Muhammad ibn Al-Habib tells us in his diwan that in the dhikr of the Rabb is the cure. This implies that to be human is to be in a state of loss or a state of suffering, and the only cure for that suffering is to remember.

In the first instance, that remembering is, quite literally, to bring to recollection. Like if I forgot for a moment where I was supposed to go and then I remember. What you need to recollect is that Allah SWT is your benefactor. Bring to mind all the things that have been given to you that you have not earned, like the peristalsis of your gut, the popping of your synapses, the metabolizing of your breakfast. He has and continues to provide for you in a way that is truly uncountable. You also need to remember that Allah SWT will protect you. Reflect on your life and consider how many things could have gone wrong that could have killed you. Surely, this must show that you are alive because of the catastrophe that has been withheld.

When you know that this is true with of a sense of conviction, one of the implications of dhikr is that you remind yourself of that truth. It's a bit intellectual. It's a calling to mind. It's a calling to recollection that He is Ar-Rahman Ar-Raheem, He is the Lord of the two mercies. He is the Lord of the mercy which He provides or the benefactor. And He is the Lord of the mercy with which He withholds or the protector. He is the ally.

When you start feeling that you're being badly done to, remind yourself, as the old people would say, to count your blessings. Bring to mind and remember all the little things that He makes go right for you on an ongoing basis, all the time. Looking into the future, consider that there were times in your past when you were looking at a narrow aperture where it looked like things would be catastrophic. Yet there was life afterwards. Things continued. Think about people who go through wartime experiences.

Our brother, Abdi, is a great example of this. At one point, he survived a civil war with people being shot around him. I'm sure if you put yourself in the shoes of the child who was going through that experience, looking forward must have been completely hopeless. People are dying; the whole world is coming to an end. And, yet, with hindsight now, he was protected. He's here today. He's with us, a beloved family man. The fear of the child looking into the future at that point proved, in the fullness of time, not to have been entirely true. He was protected.

So, when one suffers, one has to, in the first instance, bring to mind the benevolence and the protection that you have experienced.

There is a second implication to this issue of remembering, which is, in fact, the true trick. The first step is reminding yourself of the fact that you are blessed, that your life is blessed, that you are protected, and you are nurtured. That is a kind of way station; it opens a door to another possibility.

If you convince yourself of that insight long enough and frequently enough, a piece of magic happens, and it is the magic that you seek. You cease to wish to control outcomes because you know deeply that your life is the product of an amazing set of miracles that you can't manage. And the moment you start seeing that, start seeing that first-hand, it is almost as if a piece of your being lets go of the world. You become what we now refer to as inwardly gathered.

When you no longer have such a deep need to guarantee an outcome – to guarantee the future for yourself – you can let it go. This letting go means you can trust the future to Allah SWT. Yes, we've got an awful government and, yes, the country's going to the dogs, but you know what? Even in an awful government there is love, there is blessing, things come right, and life carries on. There is always a beyond. You can let go. That letting go allows you to sink back into an experience, a feeling of operating in your chest, where your attention becomes fundamentally receptive.

In other words, the second piece of remembering is not calling to recollection an understanding or an insight. It is calling to recollection an experience. The two are related. If you remind yourself of the insight for long enough, it starts to produce an experience. In other words, if you convince yourself for long enough that there is a custodial Lord in charge of your life – that your life is blessed, that it is nurtured – you start to feel protected. You feel yourself sink back into an unassailable place in your chest.

That's an experience; that's not an insight. That's an experience like a hand on your leg on your foot. That which happens in your chest is an experience, it's a feeling. That feeling is the door to reality. Reminding yourself of the fact that you are protected is a pointer. If you follow that pointer for long enough, all of a sudden it produces an experience. The experience is the true feeling of being unassailable.

That feeling of being unassailable is because your attention is disconnected from the world, the outer project that you're trying to manage. It is completely inwardly gathered. You've shifted your engagement from being predatory to being receptive; from being in your head to being in your chest.

All the inner traditions point to the centrality of the heart. This is not a metaphor. There are two principal places in your body that you can operate from: you can operate in your head, or you can operate behind your solar plexus. If you remind yourself about the benevolence of your Rabb long enough, you stop being anxious about the future. And that dropping of the anxiety, that dropping of the need to manage the future, creates the conditions where you start to operate from your chest and not from your head. It produces a feeling that can only be described as liberation. This path is about becoming increasingly reminded, not just of the insight, but of that experience.

So, eventually, dhikr doesn't mean making a noise in Arabic. It doesn't mean reminding yourself of an insight. Dhikr means bringing to recollection an experience; bringing to recollection the experience of being inwardly gathered and of operating with receptive attention behind your chest. Because, when you do that, you don't have to believe that Allah SWT is your Rabb, you don't have to believe that there is a benefactor in charge of your life, and you don't have to believe that the whole universe is your ally. You witness it. It is no longer an assertion; it is the truth.

May Allah SWT grant us nearness to Him,
May Allah SWT grant us annihilation in Him,
May Allah SWT grant us death before we die.

Chapter 10

SELF-PITY AND DEPRESSION
Discourse 11: December 2011

Bismillah ar-rahman ar-raheem

This week there were two issues that people wanted me to explore. One was from Mr. Davidson in Melbourne, whose concern was self-pity and how one deals with it. The other question was from Rabia Tahir in Karachi, whose concern was about depression and how one deals with depression. These two things are deeply related, so I'd like to deal with them together.

One can say that depression is habitual self-pity. If one examines the character of depression, there is a sense of powerlessness. There is a sense of being overwhelmed. There is a sense of futility, a sense that you are at the mercy of forces beyond your control. The conviction of being ill-done by life or ill-done by the world is what we call self-pity. We can call the single experience of being a victim self-pity, and the state of the person who is constantly in that experience, depression. The event of self-pity is the moment; it is like weather and depression is climate. Climate is the aggregate of weather. If we say that a climate is hot, it is because every day is generally hot. So, if you have depression as a climate, it is because in every moment you feel that the universe has you in its sights. You are overwhelmed and you are the victim of forces beyond your control.

This means that if we understand this experience of being the victim, or this experience of self-pity, properly and we deal with it properly, then we will change the internal weather of the person who has that experience. The knock-on effect of that is that we will change the climate, the state of depression.

You don't intervene in anything in the big. You always intervene in the incrementally small. So, if you want to change the nature of discourtesy between people in a group, you stop the individual from being discourteous in his actions and, over time, you have a sense of courtesy. The climate is a climate of courtesy in that group of people because the individual's actions are courteous actions.

You always intervene at the level where n=1. We never intervene at the level of climate. We never intervene in the big picture. As soon as you try to intervene in the big picture, you are already making yourself helpless. Because, by definition, the big picture is the big picture - it's something overwhelming.

You can't deal with your life. It is not possible to fix your life. You can only fix the moment you're in. You can only fix the individual current transaction or an individual engagement. And, so too, you can't fix depression. What you can do, where you can intervene, is to challenge your self-pity in the moment that you're in. And if you consistently challenge your self-pity in the moment that you're in and just incrementally shift it, then you experience that you are less and less depressed.

It is very appropriate to use the distinction and the idiom of climate and weather to describe what we're saying because we create inner weather, and we create inner climate. How you think about your life produces a chemical response in your body that habituates your body to a particular set of chemicals. There is a blood chemistry to depression. If you are a very heavy smoker, then it takes some time to get the nicotine out of your system once you stop smoking cigarettes. So, if you are a person who habitually feels sorry for yourself, you could stop today, but it would take a while for the climate of depression to change.

While the single instance of feeling like a victim is the only place where you can intervene, don't expect your depressed state to change instantly because it won't. Your depressed state is a chemical climate that you've created in your body. You might still be a little blue when you wake up in the morning; you may still have that lethargy that we feel when we are depressed. One has to be patient.

Now let's go to the problem itself. In the first instance, we have to accept that you can only deal with self-pity by making a non-negotiable assertion to yourself. This assertion is that all assumptions of being badly done to are false. It is not allowing yourself any breathing space for this issue of self-pity. You may say that this is unrealistic. You may think, 'You can't say that because somebody has been rude to me', or 'My spouse has been awful to me', or 'My children did not greet me this morning'. Something has hammered in that it really was unfair. You are not making it up.

When we say you have to challenge the issue of self-pity radically, it means that you always have to assert that there has to be more blessing than curse to your life, otherwise you could not be alive. That has to be fundamentally true. If more things in your life went wrong than went right, you would be dead. If you want to do justice to the big picture, you can only ever be grateful. And the antidote to self-pity is gratitude.

This is the case because self-pity says, 'I have been badly done in. I have no reason to be grateful. I have not been given my due'. On the other hand, gratitude says: 'No, no. I've been given in excess of my due. I can never repay what I have been given'.

That gratitude is not possible if you do not assert to yourself or bear witness to yourself that there is a greater genius: a God. That Allah SWT is in charge of this universe. Because the problem is just this. If you say that your life is just the outcome of an absolutely blind series of accidents, then who's there to be grateful to? In fact, if you think that your life is the outcome of a series of blind accidents, then what you're really asserting is that there isn't a protective genius that's in charge of the universe that you're in, that this is entirely random. In other words, you have to look after yourself.

That sense of having to rely on yourself means that the only way you can survive is to compete. You apprehend the world to be hostile to you. When your world is hostile to you, you will feel sorry for yourself. How could you not feel sorry for yourself when you look at that vast and overwhelming thing out there and think that it is oblivious to you and therefore dangerous to you?

This suggests that depression is an expression of kufr of a kind. It is an expression of the experience of the world that says, 'This is all random. There is no meaning to this'. That there's nothing to be grateful for.

It's very important that the thoughts that carry this view that we are alone and under threat are very subtle. This persists at a subliminal level that we are not conscious of. This suggests that a moralistic take on the problem isn't helpful. I sometimes get depressed. We all have instances of self-pity. That means we all have brushes with kufr. It is not just the kaafir that wrestles with kufr. It's not just the hard-bitten Darwinian atheist that wrestles with kufr. We all do.

Our competitiveness is basically associated with a view of the survival of the fittest. It is a view that says 'I'm going to fight. I've got to look after myself'. This does violence to the truth. This assertion that things only survive because they compete is false. Is it not obvious that deeper than the competition of individual things, there is an overall symbiosis?

Yes, the lions and the buck compete. But, at a deeper level, the buck feeds the lion, and the lion keeps the buck's population in check. In other words, there's a conscious genius that produces a big picture, which is a symbiotic picture, not a competitive picture. It's that deep sense of symbiosis that you have to claim for yourself with the radical assertion that, 'My self-pity is false'.

The truth is that there is a greater One in charge of this universe. Otherwise, I can't account for the fact that I'm still here. I am presented with a vast universe, and I am tiny. It is the nature of that which is vast to overwhelm the tiny. This universe also appears to display infinite randomness. But, if this was true, then there are an infinite number of things that could kill me right now. So why am I still here? Why have I not been overwhelmed? It has to be because vastness is not random. It is my ally. It is not random toward me. It is deliberate with regard to me, and that deliberateness operates in my interest. There is a Rabb. A custodial guardian Lord who is my benefactor and ally.

You cannot, out of your own genius, account for your life. You, as an individual, haven't created you. There have been generations of human beings that have gone before you. There's been the whole of the universe that participated in making you. So, your life is a product of other than you. Other than you is not your enemy, it's your friend; it's given you your life. Not recognizing that there is an incredibly brilliant design that has produced your life is to fly in the face of what's obvious.

Those two insights refer to Allah SWT's attributes of ar-rahman ar-raheem: the benevolent, the sustaining, and the giving; and that which withholds, the merciful. Recognizing them requires an uncompromising assertion to yourself that your self-pity has no basis. It is fundamentally false.

So, in dealing with your self-pity, you require a sort of intolerance of it. There's a piece to this which is commanding yourself to pick up your bed and walk. Stop snivelling. Stop feeling sorry for yourself. It really is as simple as that. Stop indulging. It is beneath you.

The problem we face in attempting this is the waswasa - the whispering in the chest which creeps up from behind. You had a fantastic morning, then you're in the traffic and some taxi cuts you off and the internal muttering starts. And then you're walking to an office and some person you know does not greet you. Then the elevator you get into stops at every floor, so by the time you get to the floor you are going to, you are ready to throw yourself off the top of the building. We lay up our victimhood in little increments that creep up on us.

Once you recognize that it has happened, you've got to cut through it radically. The moment you realize that you are now on a rollercoaster of negative musing, you need to say to yourself, 'Hold on. I'm now feeling depressed. I'm now feeling sorry for myself. I'm feeling that the world is nasty. This is a falsehood. I challenge myself on this. I will not allow myself to be like this. Allah SWT is generous to me. My life has more blessings than curses. The universe is not hostile to me because, if it was, I would be dead. ar-rahman ar-raheem is the truth of my life'.

Whenever you become aware of your self-pity, whenever you become aware that you're depressed, you will, step-by-step, start experiencing a change in the climate of your own blood chemistry. It'll be a little bit less depressed. A little bit more hopeful. A little bit more optimistic. A little bit more grateful. Enlightened.

The next challenge is how to shorten the cycle. We all go through cycles, but sometimes the cycles are very long. You look up again and six months have gone by, and you can't remember having had a hearty laugh in the last six months. You can't help but feel depressed.

We make the cycles long because we do not reflect enough. To reflect means to stand outside of our day and to ask what it was like being me today. This is the practice we've been speaking about as journaling. It's very important to journal. You can journal in one of two ways. You can use the journal as an opportunity to just dump your experience of the day, which is helpful because it is cathartic. However, then you're just using it as a place where you record the ills that have been done to you and can become a way of concentrating your resentment and not addressing it.

A better way of using a journal is not to comment on the world, but to comment on what it was like to be in your skin today. Were you content or discontented? Did you feel secure or insecure? Did you feel powerful or weak? Did you have a sense of harmony with the world around you, or were you in conflict? If the answer to those four questions was that you felt a bit insecure, you were discontented, there was a conflict in your day, or you felt a little bit under threat, then the next question to ask yourself is: Why?

The challenge is not to justify that you are being unjustly treated, but to challenge yourself as to whether, in the big picture, you really are being unjustly treated. It is to replace the narrative that they haven't given you your due with the question of whether Allah SWT has given you your due. If you assert that your Rabb has not given you your due today, you're shameless. How can you say that your Rabb hasn't given you your due? Did you produce the chemistry that helped you metabolize the food you ate? Did you create all the things that made it possible for you to open your eyes and be awake this morning? If Allah SWT was unkind to you, you would not be here. Alhumdullilah.

Even if the worst possible thing happened to you, it is still a blessing. If it so happened that you died and were no longer here, that would also be His kindness to you. Your suffering is at an end. Alhumdullilah. Because that's His nature. He only created us out of a love to be known. That means that what's at the root of this whole experience of life is love. It is ecstasy. It is delight. It is joy. It is not dark depression or disapproval, sour faces and stern looks, or big turbans.

So, I caution myself; I caution all of us to be deliberate about the day. To watch your experience of being in your skin like a hawk. In the first instance, be brutally honest with yourself. When you experience a depressed day, admit to yourself that you were depressed. Don't hide from this in some misplaced Islamic political correctness. The scorpion on top of the rock is far safer than the scorpion under the rock.

Once you recognize it, use it as a caution for yourself. Say 'Well, little scorpion, why are you here? What has fed you?' When you discover why you feel like this, challenge those reasons. Call them out for the falsehoods they are, until falsehood disappears in the light of truth. And the light of truth is this: there is an Allah SWT. There is a creative genius. This universe is not arbitrary, it is not random, or a set of mistakes as the kuffar tells us. You are in the custody of a custodian who has the deepest, kindest, most loving regard for you. Who protects you? Who makes every atom and causes every electron around every atom of your body to oscillate correctly so that you can live? You can rest in that hand, in the hand of your Rabb.

May Allah SWT grant us nearness to Him,
May He grant us annihilation in Him,
May He grant us death before we die.

Chapter 11

THE CONNECTIONS THAT MATTER
Discourse 12: 31 August 2019

Bismillah ar-rahman ar-raheem

Allah SWT tells us that if you expended all the wealth in the world, you could not unite or connect two hearts. And yet He connects them. He is the great. He is the wise, the knowing. There's great comfort in knowing this because we spend so much of our lives seeking to build connections with people, seeking to develop alliances, and being concerned about our circle of friends and acquaintances, not realizing that the connections that matter will happen.

They won't happen by your planning and your ingenuity. They'll happen by Allah SWT. This also implies that the alienations that are going to happen - and they will happen - will also happen by Him. The connections that matter are by Him and the losses that matter are by Him. One way of looking at the journey that we're on is that it's a process of preparing, a process of production.

Imagine some kind of manufacturing process that produces a very complex product at the end, which requires things to be put in, things to be taken out, things to be combined, and things to be separated incrementally over a period of time to produce this unique product.

The most unique product in the universe is the single human being. It's taken an immense mixing of elements over an incalculable period of time to make the human being possible. Most of that has happened before your individual life. However, the making of you is clearly not just a physiological event because who are you? You are a point of observation. You're a place, a vantage point, that can look out on existence.

You are a unique vantage point. You have been given the propensity to see things in a way that only you can see. There's a generic way in which human beings see existence, and then there's an individual way in which the human being sees existence. It's taken all the events from the beginning of time to lay down the conditions for the vantage point of a human being to be there. The preparation for the unique vantage point of an individual human being is the product of the biographic detail, the events that happened in a person's life.

By Him, you are connected by people over time, people are brought into your life over time. And, by Him, people are removed over time. They may be removed by death, they may be removed by conflict or alienation in the relationship, or they may be removed just by a simple drifting apart. What is true is that people will come, and people will go.

It doesn't serve us to be nostalgic about those we have lost. It is like a man driving to a destination and then being nostalgic because the midway point has been passed. One needs to keep both the front door and the back door of your life wide open. You need to be able and willing to accept new allies, alliances, and connections of the heart, and you have to be willing to let old ones go, without rancour, without ill feeling, without accusation, and without a sense of victimhood.

Just like people will be brought into your life because they are bringing something to you, when those alliances no longer serve you, those people will go. This is all part of the alchemy of the making of you. The journey that you go on of meeting and parting, meeting and parting, is a tempering process that finally produces this very finely honed observer; an observer like no other. This observer has a unique perspective that only this observer can offer life.

The unique place we witness from makes a unique view possible. There is an aspect of being that will and can only be apprehended from that unique vantage point. Not only are we here to witness and bear witness that He is stupendous, but we are also here to witness and bear witness that the particular view we have been honed to perceive is stupendous. He is not just stupendous in principle; He is stupendous to me, in particular. The way in which I get to see that He is the most sublime, He is the most wise, and He is the most extraordinary is the reason for my being created. It is why I am here.

Our endeavour of wanting to maintain and develop alliances is because we suffer an assumption that we can actually handle our lives, that we can be in charge of our lives, that we can manage the affair. You can no more manage the affair of your life than what a grain of sand can withstand in a tsunami.

I pray that Allah SWT brings to us those people who are going to enable us.

I pray that Allah SWT grants us the fortitude and the courage to lose those alliances that need to go.

I pray that Allah SWT liberates us from our own sentimentality, our weakness, and our self-pity.

I pray that He grants us the ability to see the blessing in all things because we know that, when we see the blessing in all things, the blessing of all things becomes available to us.

Chapter 12

THE EXOTERIC AND THE ESOTERIC UNDEFINED
Discourse 13: 1 December 2012

Bismillah ar-rahman ar-raheem

The division between the esoteric and the exoteric is an issue for all religions. The exoteric is concerned with the outward form of the religion and the esoteric is concerned with the inner experience. This same division, we know, is operative in Islam. It has created a history which has sometimes been violent and murderous, so much so that one wonders what the root is of this animosity. How is it that two men who stand shoulder to shoulder in the masjid have such different views on the matter that they could come to blows when they go outside? It occurs to me that one of the key reasons for this is these two inhabit different worlds and have irreconcilable views of creation.

The exoteric view of creation looks at creation as an artefact and Allah SWT as the divine artisan. The people of the inner view creation as theatre and Allah SWT as the director, audience, scriptwriter, and actually the essence of the actors. This became apparent to me after listening to Shaykh Muhammad Harun on a number of occasions where he described life as theatre, as a play of some kind, and all of us are actors, asked to play a role.

When you look at existence as theatre, you're not looking at existence as an artefact. When you see existence as an artefact and Allah SWT as the great artisan or artificer, it makes him removed in extremity. He is on the other side of the sky. He stands external to us and moulds us from the outside in. If you view existence as theatre, then, in a sense, He is far more intimately involved in the process. He is not an external moulder of objects from the outside, like a potter. He is the one who creates from the inside. He is inside the actor. He is inside the script. He is inside the audience.

So, the first thing that becomes apparent in these two different ways of looking at creation is that the people of the outward view creation as being constructed from the outside in. If you view existence as theatre, then you view things as being created from the inside out. Like an infant. Like a foetus. You don't get the skin first. You get the inside, the spine, and the skull. The child is constructed from the inside out.

If you have an outside in view of creation, then it's the form that matters because it's the externality that is significant. It will therefore be very important how long the trousers are, how short the beard is, that the fingernails are trimmed, and all of that. That becomes the important issue because it's the externality. It is how the thing appears to be.

From our point of view, it is the inner reality that's the important thing. That is what accounts for the sincerity of the matter, the truth of the matter. Who you are, in terms of your behaviour and in terms of how you interact as a person, is judged by your intention, and your intention is your inner reality. The inwardness produces the outwardness. It's not the other way around. Things are created inside out, not outside in.

When you view life from this point of view, it becomes apparent that Allah SWT is deeply intimate in the entire creative process. In a sense, this whole universe is a dance, and He is both the audience and the dancer. He has set your life up as a display for His enjoyment. This means that the depth of your inside, the place that your action stems from, is Him. And who you are in essence, and what produces you in essence, comes directly from Him.

This introduces a further variable: the significance of the heart. We've had a number of conversations about this. Again, I'd like to share and quote Shaykh Muhammad Harun, who frequently refers to the heart. Last night, we spoke about this, and he indicated that the heart refers to a sense of deep conviction, when you stop dithering, when you know that this is right, and this is what I must do.

When that sense of conviction comes over you, it comes from your chest. It is not a reasoned explanation in your head. When that happens, you're no longer the actor because the action that follows comes from

His hand. Then you are being produced inside out from your chest, not outside in. What shapes you then is not convention; it is not what you think appropriate behaviour may be and what people might like. What shapes you is your deep conviction of what is the right thing to do now. What does your Rabb want from you now?

When you're being shaped by convention, you're being shaped from the outside in. The problem with allowing yourself to be shaped outside in is that you lose your life, eventually. You become a shadow of the man - a shell, a husk. You only have a face. You only have a persona, a mask. You don't have this sense of authenticity that comes out of the chest.

It, therefore, stands to reason that there should be hostility between the people of the inner and the people of the outer, and that the people of the outer would experience the people of the inner as fundamentally rebellious. On the other hand, the people of the inner would experience the people of the outer as fundamentally oppressive, as being concerned with that which is arbitrary, that which is insignificant and superficial, and that which is purely concerned with form and externalities.

Now, Allah SWT has probably set this theatre up like this so that we can understand who we are. It is not appropriate to tolerate the people of the outer world in a spirit of animosity or ill feeling. If they were not there, we would not be able to be clear about how we see things. They provide the necessary foil to clarify our perception. If there wasn't this sense out there that it is all about form, then we would not grapple with the issue of essence. These people are our buddies. They are the sparring partners who tease us into finding the depth of the matter. If you didn't have people getting completely lost in the myriad of rules and sub-rules which concern externalities, then, in a sense, we wouldn't have something to kick against; we wouldn't have the counterpoint.

It is not appropriate to bear these people ill will. Understand that their way of being makes another way of being possible for you. The essence of what that struggle makes possible for you is claiming for yourself the right to the divine encounter. Your Rabb is not outside of you. He is not the artificer on the other side of the clouds putting you together. He is the intimate insider. As He says Himself: He is closer to you than your jugular vein. He is the inside of your inside. He built you inside out.

If you allow him to build you inside out, he makes you a magnificent being. Because when anything is real rather than artificial, it is robust. It is magnificent. It is beautiful. It has a natural wholesomeness to it. Why is it that when you walk into a house and you see a nice flower arrangement, the first thing you do is go feel it? If you discover that it is made from plastic, you have an immediate sense of disappointment. On the other hand, when you feel that it is a real flower, you have an immediate sense of delight. Why? Because, at depth, we have an aversion to the artificial flower. Because the plastic is fake, and we don't want the fake. We want the real. We don't want just the image, the externality, the outside, the form. We want the inside.

When you allow yourself to become like a plastic flower, you really cease to be interesting. You have no aroma. You can't be savoured. What makes a flower so special is not just what you see out there, but how it can become intimately part of you. It can become intimately part of you through other senses: through touch and through smell. When you're smelling, then, suddenly, it's no longer only in the flower. The flower has gone into your olfactory nerves, into your insides. It's gone into your head. It's in your lungs. It has become part of you.

When someone really allows themselves to be from the inside out, you can savour them. They become enjoyable. You don't have to necessarily like the person, but there is just something about that person that is special. This is because there is authenticity in that person. That person is radiating from the inside out. They are allowing their Rabb to make them. They're not just mechanically dancing to your convention. They are not trying to assimilate in external form.

They've been made rooted in their spontaneity, from the inside out. They have a deep sense of what's appropriate. Often, these people are also sometimes unpredictable because they do what is right; they don't do what is conventional.

In this century of the plastic. The convention has gone so extreme that people of belief will literally spill blood because of an issue around the size of a headscarf. We owe it to ourselves to become deeper and bigger than that. We owe it to ourselves to have our own lives. Why settle for a plastic existence? Why settle for the purely superficial and the purely conventional? Why settle for a sham? You've got to live your life anyhow; you may just as well live it for real.

If you crack this code, it is the end of your suffering. You might still have physical discomfort, but the heart of your suffering - your grief about what you've lost and your terror of what's coming towards you - will all go away. Your Rabb promises you that because you have left the matter with him. You've allowed Him to make you inside out.

May Allah SWT grant us nearness to Him,
May He grant us annihilation in Him,
May He grant us death before we die.

Chapter 13

THE TWO APPLICATIONS OF THE DEEN
Discourse 14: 3 August 2019

Bismillah ar-rahman ar-raheem

There are two applications of the deen; two ways of being Muslim in the world. The first application of the deen is about identity. It is about self-consciously becoming Muslim, articulating a Muslim identity, describing yourself as a Muslim, and deliberately allying yourself with the community of the faithful that we refer to as the Umma. It is about fitting in and joining in. This is a perfectly legitimate application of the deen. There is no harm in it.

There is, however, a second application of the deen, which is to see your deen as a technology of transformation. You see your deen to be a method by which you can grow spiritually to the point where you have an experience of the divine encounter.

What we have to understand about these two applications of deen is that, while there is no judgement of one or the other, they are mutually exclusive. You cannot pursue the divine encounter while you are articulating your deen as an identity because, unfortunately, the divine encounter comes at the price of the loss of identity. On the path, we refer to that loss of identity as fanaa fillah or the annihilation of the self in Allah SWT.

Further, our endeavour on this path is the latter. It is the divine encounter. That's what we're trying to do here. We're not trying to gain another identity. While it is perfectly legitimate to accept and take on your deen as identity and we have no judgement of people who do that, we are, at the same time, very careful not to be too self-conscious about identifying ourselves as members of a club.

Throughout the centuries, the people of this path have been notoriously open. They have been able to sit comfortably with anybody and drink from knowledge wherever they find it. The people of this path have had the ability to take from whatever source they could find. So, if you examine the tasawwuf of South Asia, it looks and feels Hindu. The tasawwuf of Central Asia looks and feels Shamanic. The tasawwuf of Anatolia feels Greek. The tasawwuf of North Africa feels Berber. We use whatever we can find. The people of tasawwuf are notoriously fickle in terms of what they are willing to take and use. We steal everybody's stuff. This is because the issue is not the map. The issue is to experience the territory.

Another way of understanding the difference between people who pursue the deen as identity and people who pursue deen as a path to the divine encounter is that the people who pursue the deen as identity are cartographers. They are map makers. Whereas the people who pursue the deen as transformation are far more interested in the territory than in the map. We want the experience; we don't want the description of the experience.

How often does one find people who could give very erudite discourses quoting volumes from Bukhari or reams from Muslim in fluent Arabic, and yet don't really understand what they're talking about in terms of first-hand experience? On the other hand, sometimes you can sit with a very simple person who knows none of this stuff, and you can sense that this person knows. This person really knows. They are close to their Rabb.

I say again, the pursuit of the knowledge of the cartographers is perfectly legitimate, but it is not our pursuit here. Our pursuit is the taste. Our pursuit is the first-hand experience of Allah SWT. Presence.

And we know that that experience is possible. We know that that closeness is a reality that it can be experienced as a first-hand reality.

May Allah SWT grant us nearness to Him,
May He grant us annihilation in Him,
May He grant us death before we die.

Chapter 14

THE MUSLIM IDENTITY
Discourse 15: 26 October 2013

Bismillah ar-rahman ar-raheem

Nusrat recited Surah Ikhlas and, in it, Allah SWT reminds us that He is singular and there is none like Him. In that reminder, He tells us that, beneath and beyond this world of phenomenal form that we experience, where things apparently exist as separate things, there is a continuity, which is His nature, threaded through all things.

It also means that to see difference is to appraise things superficially. The more cosmetic and superficial your understanding and experience of things is, the more you will see things as being irreconcilable and different. It also implies that the deeper you go, the more sameness and continuity you see. Here we are sitting in a room. We're different. We have different skin types, and we have different cultural backgrounds. And yet, based on a single conviction alone, that Allah SWT has given us our Rasul (s.a.w.s.) who has brought us this message, we are the same. The difference we see is apparent. It hides a deeper continuity.

However, in this majlis today, we also hosted people who were not Muslim. There were some people who I know were outright kuffar. And what I mean by that is that they weren't Christians or Jews or even fire-worshipers. They actually believe that there is no greater genius to existence; they are complete deniers of the truth. And yet, if you strip their conviction that there's no greater genius behind all things and we strip your conviction that there is, what is there? We're just the same. Each one of us is a frightened little being, standing on this very rickety scaffold of a body, looking out on this vast, infinite, absolutely unfathomable, and stupendous universe.

When we strip all our pretences away, all that is superficial (and by the way that also includes the claim to be Muslim), who are you, really? Who is this scintillating, magical being that Allah SWT brought into the world that incrementally decided that I'm a man, a girl, a boy, Malay, Indian, Muslim, Christian, or a kaafir. Before all of that happened, who were you?

You have to understand that our path is about discovering who you originally were before you became hooked onto an identity. Before you somehow thought that, because you can mutter some words in Arabic and you wear a headscarf, you're somehow significant.

This is clearly a very contentious thing to say. It's very contentious to say that there's something deeper to you than your Islamic identity, but that is indeed the truth. You see, all the things that we do that are concerned with being Muslim are really concerned with being identified as a Muslim. If it is about being identified as a Muslim, then it is about your identity as a Muslim. And if it is about your identity as a Muslim, it's not about who you are on the inside; it's about who you are seen to be, who you're identified as. By whom? By someone other than you.

To be Muslim is to be the one who has submitted. The one who has submitted is the one whose being is in sajda. The one whose being is in sajda has no identity because he has put his face on the ground. And when your face is on the ground, you look the same as any other human being. You have no identity.

The reason why we try to escape this identity of being a Muslim, and indeed any identity, is because we want to discover what our real nature is. Because you have to understand that the degree to which you are alienated from your real nature, the degree to which you are not acting consistently with your real nature, is the degree to which you suffer. All of your suffering - every single element of discontentment, of insecurity, of feeling threatened by other than you, of conflict with the world around you - is based on your assumption that you exist separate from the world; that you are somehow significant and apart from others.

On this path, we are not seeking to be particularly holy, or particularly significant or different. On this path, we pursue what it means to be truly human - this deeper reality that we were given by our Rabb, that we've somehow tarnished into this diversion of being significant. Allah SWT has made a huge investment in you. From the beginning of time, from the Big Bang, He's been putting together and weaving together the conditions to make your being possible. And now, finally, millions of years after the first event, here you are.

This immense investment, all this weaving together of stuff, was done to produce you now. To make you possible. So now you are here. What is the point of you being here? Is the point of you being here to be significant? To consider yourself to be superior to others, beyond others, and greater than others?

If you consider that the reason why you're here is to be significant and to be seen, you are reneging on the first contract. The first contract is to recognise that He is incalculable, stupendous, and vast beyond description. His contract with you is that you will find Him breathtaking, that you will find Him extraordinary, and that you will find Him supremely significant. Allahu akbar. La ilaaha illallah: there's nothing that's significant other than Allah SWT. He is the one to be raised above all. He is the one to be seen and appraised. He is the significant one, not you, madam or mister Muslim in your peculiar cultural attire, wishing to be noticed for being Muslim.

The degree to which you wish to be noticed is the degree to which you are blind. The one who wishes to be seen does not see. How can you see the stupendous nature of your Rabb, when you are so caught up in your own significance, in your own standing up, in your own importance? Just as the eye which sees itself is blind, so too is the I.

Understand that your Islamic identity is purely a device to remind you of who the Rabb is. It is a pulpit that you stand on; it is not something to be worshipped. It is a vehicle, not a destination. It is not absolute. Allah SWT alone is absolute. Do not turn your Islamic identity into an idol. When you do, you are no different from the kaafir who sat in this majlis today.

We are the same. We face the same examination. We face the same grave. We do battle with the same set of issues. We also suffer the same misery, based on the degree to which we do not make the object of our life He who is beyond language, He who is beyond description, He who is breathtaking and stupendous.

Alhumdullilah.

May Allah SWT grant us nearness to Him,
May Allah SWT grant us annihilation in Him,
May Allah SWT grant us death before we die.

Chapter 15

THE PURPOSE OF OUR BROKENNESS
Discourse 10: 4 July 2015

Bismillah ar-rahman ar-raheem

Allah SWT, our Rabb, is the most compassionate. This has to mean that He also is uniquely and personally compassionate. He is personally compassionate to our own individual frailty and our own individual suffering. And we are so frail. And we do suffer so much with the disappointments and sadness that we carry on through our lives.

I was gifted today with a video of a qawwali recital somewhere in Sindh, Pakistan. And, although I found the music very attractive and wonderful, what was more interesting were the faces of some of the fuqaraa' in the crowd. You could see brokenness in all of them, literally: broken teeth, haggard faces, and thin bodies. Suffering and yet ecstatic.

Imam Kamardine recited from the Qur'an, 'Verily in your suffering, there's ease'. I've heard this interpreted in two different ways: either after your suffering there's ease, or in the suffering there's ease. This second sense of ease lies in our frailty because it's our frailty and our brokenness that give us our uniqueness.

If you examine goods coming off a production line, when they are whole, they each resemble one another. But it's the one that fell off the production line – that got broken, and then got kind of clumsily put back together – that is the one that is unique. It is unique because of its brokenness.

And that is true for us. We all came off this production line of becoming human. Clean. Fresh from the presence of our Rabb. And we got dashed against the rocks of our lives and were broken. But that's exactly what makes us special. It is that frailty which creates the possibility of your unique engagement with your Rabb. Allah SWT is, for you, the exact inverse of this brokenness, outwardly.

Where you are frail, He is whole. Where you are finite, He's infinite. Where you are incapable, He is capable. Where you are weak, He is mighty. He's the exact invert, the exact opposite – like a daguerreotype or a photograph that is just the outline. He encapsulates you totally. However, this is not an abstract principle. He is not the mirror fit to frailty. He's the mirror fit to *your* frailty.

You are broken in such a way that only He can heal you. Because only He is the invert, the absolute mirror opposite. The fit. And that is the purpose of your brokenness. The purpose of your brokenness is so that you can have this ecstatic homecoming. If you consider how we look at conjugal relationships, there's always this physiologically driven need to be requited. I need to connect physically. I need to have my mirror - my invert that I can merge with, become one with, whole with.

But, as we know, that thing makes a greater promise than it can deliver. Although it comes with the initial sense of completion, it is followed by a whole ocean of inadequacy and suffering. Any person who's married who claims they've made their marriage work doesn't know what they're talking about. If your marriage works, it is because there is some miraculous ingenuity at work. You can't make this thing work. You can just do the very best you can and hope that Allah SWT brings it through.

So rather than being a source of self-pity, our brokenness can also be a source of deep joy. It is the lack, the incompleteness, that creates the possibility of the completion that only He can complete. There are several implications for this.

The first is obviously that we need to be patient with our own frailty. That does not suggest that you indulge your weaknesses at all. It does not give you a license to misbehave.

Being patient with your frailty is to be patient with your suffering. All the little sadnesses, the unrequitedness, that lost love, that dashed aspiration - these things are all the special bits that make you. Nobody will quite have that special sad bitterness relating to that goal that you lost, or that career opportunity, or that business that went belly up, or whatever. That is yours, uniquely.

You need to be patient with that. You need to be patient with that because you need to know that this is the anvil of your life against which Allah SWT, as the hammer, has beaten you to create your flaws, to create your cracks, so that He can complete you. So that you can, at the end of your life, attest that He is the source of fulfilment and of happiness.

The second implication to this is not just having patience with yourself and your own frailty, but also having patience with the frailty of others. We're very quick to march in and command and correct and fix: 'This should be like that, like so, like this'. The more appropriate thing to do is to look at the frailty and the brokenness of those around you with a compassionate eye. To recognise, 'There, but for the grace of God, go I'.

In fact, let's rephrase that: 'There, because of the grace of God, I have been'. Because that person manifests their frailty in one way, and you manifest in something else. That doesn't make that person less or more significant than you. Or you are more significant than them.

To claim not to be cracked is the greatest shirk. This is the greatest arrogance. Then you're saying you're exempt from the process of becoming human. You are self-sufficient. Your brokenness is your in-self-sufficiency. If you claim that you are so okay - that you are beyond judgement - then you're claiming self-sufficiency to yourself. That is shirk. That is the greatest discourtesy to Allah SWT, your creator. It is unacceptable. The appropriate engagement with those around us, and with the world around us, is not an engagement with the intent to fix, but an engagement with the intent to suffer with. The Afrikaans word for this is 'medeleiding'. It is the direct translation of the English word compassion but suggests something a bit different. Or, at least, it means what the word compassion can be deconstructed to mean. 'Passion' means suffer, and 'com' means with: suffering with.

That means you can hold somebody else's frailty with respect and recognise your own frailty in somebody else's frailty. Holding their frailty with respect is like a du'a that brings the nasrallah, or the help of Allah SWT, quicker than you fixing them. You can fix nothing. You, yourself, are broken. Who are you intending to fix?

So, hear them out. Listen to their brokenness with no other intention other than to listen to their brokenness.

While you are hearing them out, have your heart open like two hands in du'a. Ask Allah SWT, 'Ya Rabb, grant this soul healing like I require healing. Because, truly, you are the releaser. You are the one with the key. You're the one with the answers. You are the cure, and I remain the bereft. I remain inadequate. I remain your docile, submitted, and subordinate slave'.

That's the proper station of the human being. The one with the soft eye. The one who's somewhat bemused. The one who holds their own frailty and the frailty of others in a very gentle hand. In a hand that's so gentle that just the attention of holding it heals – without an intention to fix.

May Allah SWT grant us nearness to Him,
May He grant us annihilation in Him,
May He grant us death before we die.

Chapter 16

THE PATH OF THE FUQARAA'
LEADS OUT OF THE CITY
Discourse 16: 9 May 2020

Bismillah ar-rahman ar-raheem

If we contrast the raw and the cooked, the wild and the tamed, the world of the citizen and the world of the nomad and the wild frontiersman, then the being of the faqeer is far more consistent with the raw, the wild, and untamed than it is with the sedate, conventional, and compliant world of the city.

To be a faqeer is to pursue the divine encounter. This does not make us unique or special. It makes us a part of a torrent of humanity who has committed themselves to this endeavour from the beginning of the human story. You get mysticism in all the great religions of the world. What all mystics agree on is that we are seeking an experience of the divine which is beyond the transactional and the conventional.

You see, there is a disquiet, an existential disquiet, that lies behind the conventional good behaviour of the citizen. Their good behaviour is part of a contract, which is engaged with other citizens and the city, that says that if I behave myself, you will do the same, and we will all get on famously together. More so, we will provide for each other and protect each other. And so, we engage in these patterns of reciprocal mediocrity, which keep each other all nice and predictable, defined, and safe. The problem is that most of us find this unspeakably boring. We also suspect that is fundamentally false.

The worldview of the citizen is founded on a lie, which is that you don't own your life and you don't own your right to be. You've been granted your life and you've been granted who you are absolutely free and completely unconditionally by the most stupendous benefactor, who is not engaging in a transaction with you. There's nothing for you to reciprocate.

The human being who has fundamentally taken that truth to heart is likely to be experienced as fickle and unpredictable in terms of the normal games of reciprocity.

This is true for all mystics. A Catholic example is that of Saint Francis of Assisi. Before he engaged in what he saw as his mission, Saint Francis was a member of a very wealthy family in Assisi. He was heir apparent to his father. He was going to take over the family business. However, he kept on doing really outrageous things, like spending family funds on restoring derelict churches and giving his wealth to the poor.

This got to the point where his father had a legal case against Saint Francis with the bishop of Assisi. In that confrontation, Saint Francis took his clothes off, threw them at the feet of his father and said, 'There, I have nothing from you anymore'. In medieval Europe, to be naked was a very shameful thing. This flouting of convention was him breaking with convention and reneging on being a dutiful member of the merchant class of Assisi.

Saint Francis spent the rest of his life in abject poverty. He spent the rest of his life administering to the most downtrodden and rejected people of the society, living among lepers, and feeding wild animals. He lived completely outside of the norm. He also did not live very long. This was clearly not a very healthy lifestyle. But that is exactly the point you see.

The pursuit of the divine requires a metaphorical casting away of your clothes. This path demands a metaphorical throwing up, a casting off of your position, your class, and your privilege. If you see any Sufi who's worth his salt, that person will always have a sniff of notoriety around them. There will always be a hint of infamy concerning the person. It's always like that.

In fact, when you encounter a person who claims to be on this path who doesn't have this element of the trickster, be highly suspicious because there's some duplicity going on there. The Sioux, the Native Americans otherwise known as the Lakota, recognize people who have this quality. They refer to these people as tricksters and they are required to do things like wear bizarre clothing, wear peculiar hats, put their shoes on the wrong feet, and wear their clothing back to front. If it's a man, it would not be unusual for them to wear a woman's dress; they just constantly break the norm. It is understood that those who are closer to the divine will not conform to the norm.

If we say that the path of the fuqaraa' leads out of the city, it also leads to a place which is the singular engagement of the vastness of what's out there, in solitude. The highest points for the people of tasawwuf are not points of communion, they're points of solitude. Why do we make such a fuss and performance about the khalwa? It is because we understand that the divine encounter is the product of seclusion and removal, of being secreted in caves and woods.

If you examine the history of North African tasawwuf, some of the greatest shaykhs were people whose behaviour could only be described as abnormal. Shaykh Abu Madyan is the father of much of the North African tasawwuf. We have a direct line to him through the Shadhiliyya. He used to sleep on the graves of Fez. He didn't have a home. His home was somebody else's grave. He was so dysfunctional that he could not be married. He was given a wife by a shaykh and then he ran away from her.

If one is sincere about this endeavour of tasawwuf, one has to understand that, at some point, the bug bites for real. When the bug bites for real then, from that point forward, you are not the same as other people. Your heart longs for the heather, for the wilderness, for solitude. You are aimed out of the compact of good behaviour, which defines the citizens.

On this journey out of the city, your Rabb will present you with challenges, which will cause you to do what you deeply see as correct, but at the same time will cause you to be alienated from the proper, the socially accepted, and the socially acceptable. Your fellow citizens will look at you with shock and horror. They will not be able to understand what you're doing. At best, they'll see what you're doing as slightly seditious and, at worst, they'll see what you are doing as completely immoral and dangerous.

It is impossible to achieve the highest of your own spirit, to reap the benefit of the divine encounter, if you seek to be considered a good person. The sooner you disabuse yourself of that illusion, the easier this path becomes. And who is to say that, because they sit in judgement of you, you are wrong? It is entirely possible that the whole village will collude on what is completely fundamentally wrong.

How was it possible for the Chinese to think, for several centuries, that it was entirely acceptable to take little girls, break their feet, and bind them, so as to turn them into cripples for the rest of their lives? An entire community of people agreed on this and did the most unspeakable violence on their own children. These were good people who were doing what was agreed to be good behaviour.

Explain to me how the apartheid regime based their vindication of a completely sick political ideology on their interpretation of scripture. They had a scriptural vindication for their view. How on earth did that happen? Having grown up in that world, I can tell you that any person who would have sat comfortably like we're sitting now, as a group of mixed people, would have been seen to be perverse. Wrong. How is it at all acceptable that old women in Sudan today still do the violence of clitorectomy on young girls when they themselves know about the suffering that it caused them? That is culture. That is our culture: violence.

So thinking that the city doesn't collude around things that are fundamentally sick and perverse is naïve. The city will collude regarding things that will cause you to be cast out should you confront them. It is easy when you look at the apartheid state from the outside, or you look at societies that commit female circumcision from the outside, or when you look at Chinese foot binding from the outside, to disapprove of it. But that's not where the strength lies. The strength lies with the person who is in that society and disapproves, and will have nothing to do with it. Because it is fundamentally sick.

All the collusions are fundamentally sick because they are all based on a lie. The lie is just this: that you can provide for and protect each other. You cannot. Because there is only one provider, one protector.

You don't need to be alienated from your own sense of yourself just so that they can see that you're acceptable. That is the violence that sits underneath all violence, which all communities perpetrate. The first price of being a citizen is that you have to disavow yourself of your wildness. You've got to tame yourself. You've got to come back into the city. You've got to live in the little box and behave.

I want to say one last point about this. Where our Rabb points us in this time, and particularly through the message that we are presenting to the world through this Zawia, is that you actually have to crawl out of the city; it's no longer possible to walk out. You have to do this thing by stealth. But don't think that if you're doing it by stealth that they don't, at some point, catch on to exactly what you're doing. And that you don't then actually garner for yourself exactly the same notoriety that the whole tradition of fuqaraa' have done since the beginning of this journey.

The faqeer is the one who affirms that there's nothing other than five prayers and waiting for death. Waiting for death means you are quite comfortable with the idea that you are a corpse. Did you know that the corpse is the most objectionable thing that a human being can actually consider? So you consider yourself to be the most objectionable thing, a thing to be cast out, thrown out of the city into a hole, uncovered. That's who you are. Hold on to that and you no longer have any other pretensions. Then you are free from their tyranny.

May Allah SWT grant us nearness to Him,
May He grant us annihilation in Him,
May He grant us death before we die.

Chapter 17

OUTWARDLY SOBER, INWARDLY INTOXICATED
Discourse 17: 20 August 2019

Bismillah ar-rahman ar-raheem

Shaykh Shadhili described our path as a path of being outwardly sober and inwardly intoxicated. This dictum of outer sobriety and inner intoxication is a very eloquent description of the stealth you need to succeed on this path. We aren't the people who wander semi-naked in the marketplace and proclaim, 'Ana al-haqq!' so that our heads may be cut off. You can if you want to but, as Shadhilis, we are not enthralled by the melodramatic.

This is because we have no discomfort with the issue of compliance. Society has to happen. The children have to be made tame. They have to be civilised. They come to us raw, through the seething cauldron of bloody, beating life. They are wild beings delivered into our care to be cauterised, to be cut off from that pounding original vitality. If this violence was not done to them, they would stay wild, feral, and fundamentally dangerous to the community. The circumcision of boys is the ritual expression of this truth.

The socialising of the child is fundamentally doing violence to the child, whether you like it or not. By giving the child language, you have to alienate them from the original pristine state of connectedness with their Rabb. This is a violence, but what choice do we have? If we are not going to civilise them, there will not be a next generation.

This cutting-off is also an introduction to a really complex world of excruciating double binds, a world of oughts and shoulds. Some of them are really bizarre, like 'You must love Allah SWT'. It is like telling the child

73

you must play. Surely, love and compulsion are opposites? Surely, if my affection for you is not freely given but is compelled from me, then we are talking about a rape of a kind. This cannot be love. And yet we have no discomfort telling the child, 'You have got to love your parents'.

Alan Watts explored this problem very eloquently, this conundrum which we produce when we alienate people from their sense of spontaneity and play. The violence we do by getting people to comply. And yet, people have to comply because, if they don't, we have anarchy. What a miserable condition.

As people who want the real and the authentic, we could condemn compliance in principle. Burn the hierophants. As Pink Floyd famously sang 'We don't need no education'. We'll reinvent the whole thing: our sense of identity, our sense of morality, our idea of good order. No one is going to tell me what to believe and how to act. It is a perfectly justifiable response to being forced to comply.

That, however, comes with a disadvantage because, when you do that, you start picking a fight with the masters of compliance. This will end up in a bit of a horror show because they are many and you are few.

You will lose.

So is it possible to regain my authenticity in a way that is a bit more subtle, in a way where I am not wasting energy on unnecessary fights? Surely the bigger problem is not the external chains that are imposed on me, but the ones that sit inside me. The 'chains in my brains' that the American Black Panthers alluded to. Dealing with these internal chains requires me not to squander my limited life force on the futile endeavour of rebelling against the authorities. Isn't that how the Rasul (s.a.w.s.) described the greater struggle as the struggle within, not the struggle without?

Shaykh Shadhili told us to be outwardly sober. This means that when they look at you, they see compliance. They have no idea that sitting underneath is a drunkard. Sitting underneath this is this crazy person waiting to burn down the temple. Underneath.

They have no idea. Keep it like that.

They shouldn't have an idea. Because if they get an idea of the liberation you are actually pursuing, you are going to start wasting some of the energy that you need to do your inner work in defending yourself and justifying yourself.

You don't have to justify your pursuit of the divine encounter to anyone. It's like saying that I have to justify to somebody that I'm breathing. However, you will end up justifying yourself if you make tasawwuf your identity. So don't make it your identity. Be like them outwardly. Be outwardly sober so they don't distinguish you. Look the same. Wear the same outfit, the same beard. Because their view will be, if it appears the same, it is the same, and they will leave you alone. That's stealth. That's eloquence.

It is a deeply seditious thing we're busy with here. You only do it by stealth. You don't stand out when you do this, not because you are trying to be duplicitous, but because the way of being that we are trying to develop here is the way of stealth. You see, we do not need to have the majority of the conflicts that we have with others. When we are in conflict, we are contending. We need to put them in their place. We need to get our due. We need to rise to our own defence.

What if you knew that what is written for you was ordained before endless time by the one from whom nothing can be withheld, and from whom nothing can be compelled? If He has got that one lentil aimed at your mouth, nobody else is going to interfere to withhold it from you. You don't have to contend for your good fortune. You need not come to your defence because you have practised the art of entrusting your good auspices to the ally and the benefactor, and you have found Him to be the most trustworthy custodian of your interests.

In this world that we are in, we are taught to be contentious and contending. We've all got to appear, to stand out, to be the one who has got rights, to be the one who is noticed and is taken seriously - the one who is significant. On this path, we are cultivating a different being. Not one who does the outer struggle of appearing and contending, but the inner struggle of disappearing, of learning how to stand in, of learning how to become inwardly gathered. Not the one who occupies space, but the one who makes space.

It is only then that you can discover that your best auspices have already been guaranteed. How else are you going to know that the very best is already written for you until you stop managing the affair to get it? While you are managing the affair, even if you do get it, you congratulate yourself that it is your own effort that did it.

If you learn to do the opposite skill, which is not to try to demand or take, but to allow things to come to you, then you start to do the job that the human being was created to do. The human being was created to demonstrate that He is the one to be worshipped, that He is in charge. You demonstrate that by stopping being in charge yourself. Part of forgoing being in charge is to develop a kind of anonymity - a political anonymity - and not contending out there. If you do - if, for example, you're part of a group saving the whales - don't take the business too seriously. You know there is no utopia to be achieved out there, Islamic or otherwise.

That's not to say there isn't a place for acting in the world. There is a place for acting in the world, but most of us are so busy acting that it is the only thing we know. We behave like raging lions. We go from one confrontation to another.

We are predators. That's how Allah SWT has made us. We've got eyes in front of our heads. But actually, we should ambush predators like a leopard. A leopard sits in a tree and does very little. He yawns most of the day, until that little deer happens to sit under the wrong tree and, like lightning, it's over.

Do you live like that? Do you live like an ambush predator? When there is a confrontation, does it come out of a pool of placidity? And when it is done, do you return to the same placid state?

So, if you do have to act, act with eloquence; act with panache. If you do have to engage, come from a state of rest, go back to a state of rest. That can only happen when you develop the skill of staying inwardly gathered, which is the greater jihad. The lesser jihad is about contending in the world. If you succeed at the first, the second one is unnecessary because you don't have to contend. It comes to you.

I pray Allah SWT grants us success on this path,
that He grants us nearness to Him,
that He grants us annihilation in Him,
that He grants us death before we die.

Chapter 18

ESCAPING YOUR IDENTITY
Discourse 18: 29 May 2011

Bismillah ar-rahman ar-raheem

The first hadith in both the most accepted collections of hadith claims that the Rasul (s.a.w.s.) said that all actions are by their intention. This insight that action is only a vehicle to carry a far more significant issue, which is the issue of intention, is true in all matters. It is true in matters of deen; it is true in matters of trade; it is true in matters of family relationships. This issue of intent is the heart of the problem.

There was a young man who sought to do hijra with the Rasul (s.a.w.s.) because he wanted to marry a woman who was with the muhajireen. When this was brought to the Rasul's (s.aw.s) attention, he did not disapprove of this, but said that there are those who have gone on hijra for Allah SWT and his Rasul (s.a.w.s.), and there are those who have gone on hijra for marriage. It is the same hijra outwardly but with a completely different significance.

Our deen is no different from all other human affairs. It takes on different characters and has different significance, depending on the intent that you put into it. Intention can be classified into four basic categories. The first two can be articulated as 'I'm here to get' or 'I give to get'. In these cases, the fundamental interest of the self is self-preservation and the significance of the self.

You can be a Muslim in order to pursue that kind of intent. It's perfectly valid but not necessarily very noble. It's like the man who is the paid imam. The deen is secondary and the living is first. It is like the man who wants to be seen to have this immense eloquence, who knows many quotations, and who wears a big turban and a bigger cloak.

It reminds me of a wonderful story I heard from Shaykh Abdul Qadir once. He said he once met a man who introduced himself as 'the Grand Mufti of Odessa'. Shaykh Abdul Qadir looked at him in absolute amazement and said, 'A lot of good that has done you'.

So you can use deen to be significant, to get the attention of people in a fine robe and a turban. This will be very impressive. However, this is not our matter. From our point of view, this is contemptible and not worthy of being spoken about, precisely because it is insincere.

So, what about those who are sincere? Our tariqa is divided into three categories which Shaykh Ali al Jamal described as the common, the elite, and the elite of the elite. This classification is not derisive of the common, but it does recognise the difference between that which is common and that which is rare, and that there is a progression between them.

The deen of the common, of most Muslims who are sincere about their deen, is really about being a member of the Umma, the community of the faithful. The essential concern here is identity. It is about being seen to be part of this community and having a sense of belonging. Interestingly, this way of being has some things in common with the way of being of the insincere ones we spoke about before. They are both concerned with accumulation. The insincere one accumulates packages of learning in the form of hadith or ayat from the Qur'an to be seen to have them. They want to be noticed, to be seen to be clever.

The sincere person is also accumulating, but he is not accumulating good opinions. He is accumulating thawab, the reward from his Rabb. This person does not do things to be seen to be a good person. This person is genuinely trying to be a good person. However, when somebody is trying to be morally good, they are actually concerned with social compliance. You are still one of the community of the faithful.

This is perfectly legitimate and for one to use the word common for these people is really a bit uncharitable because it does carry a derisive value judgement. In my experience, most Muslims are like this, and it is not a selfish or a destructive way of being. Rather, it is a benign and responsible way of being, the way of being of the custodians.

What happens over time, though, is that the emphasis on content shifts to a curiosity regarding intent. Let me give you an example. In a Muslim household, for example, in Ramadan, you see all the little children around the table, half asleep, and the father is saying, 'Now you must say your niyya'. Everybody says stuff in Arabic that they don't understand. They just want to go back to bed.

Sometimes, when you ask the father himself the meaning of what he just said, he often has a very vague idea. He will only say, 'I said my niyya as I was taught to say it'. Does this not strike you as unspeakably bizarre? Niyya means intention. This man has made his intention in Arabic, a language he doesn't understand, and has taught his sleepy children to do the same. There is no intention there, there is a mouthing of a formula taught by the fathers.

Hopefully, at some point in your life, this does not satisfy you anymore. At some point in your life, you have a curiosity about what this action means. You're actually cheeky enough to say, from your heart in your mother tongue, 'Ya Rabb, today I'm going to fast for You'. Now you've made an intention. You're not repeating a formulaic thing that is being carried from generation to generation. It's you who is saying it. You are making this intention.

You have moved away from content, form, and the incidentals, to intent - to what all this really means. Which is not so much about being good Muslims, but rather about the divine encounter. From one point of view, the person who is doing salat to be a good Muslim and the person who is doing salat in the pursuit of the divine encounter are quite literally opposites. They look the same from the outside, but what is actually happening is completely different.

The first person is performing acts of worship, while still keeping time going. He is keeping time going because he is doing what he is doing as an investment in akhira, the world to come. The second person is doing the same thing not to get there in the hereafter, but to taste closeness with his Rabb now. Not tomorrow, not on the other side of the grave. Now.

The first person is holding on to and perpetuating his identity. He is doing things to be a good Muslim, to earn his place among the speakers of Arabic in janna. The second person is busy escaping his identity. This person does not view his acts of worship as acts of accumulation or investment, but acts of stripping away or divestment. In a sense, he is not trying to learn more. He is trying to unlearn so that he can see the essence of things, uncluttered by interpretation and opinion.

I want to repeat that, while these two endeavours are really mutually exclusive, there is no judgement on either. It is quite correct to be a good Muslim and to confirm your identity as being a good Muslim - to be a responsible member of the Umma, looking after your world, and investing in your hereafter. However, understand that this technology that you have of salat can do more than confirm your identity as a member of the community of the faithful. It can actually also be that path out of that community, beyond the walls of the city, into the wilderness. This is what happens when you start taking the issue of intention seriously by deliberately exercising your attention.

Identity is about being seen: 'I'm Abdallah. I'm seen'. However, to truly be Abdallah means to disappear, to forgo any will of your own and to hand over all outcomes and projects to Him, unconditionally. Your sajda can either be a statement of being Muslim, or it can be an exercise in disappearing. It can either be a confirmation of your identity, or a melting away of your identity. It can either confirm who you think you are, or it can transform you by enabling you to transcend who you think you are. The whole of deen can either be about identity or a technology of transformation.

If you view it as a technology of transformation, you can be very minimalistic about it. It is so ingenious that you need very little. You know, the earliest Muslims did not learn a lot about the Qur'an. They didn't need to. One or two ayat sufficed them because they would plumb the depths of the ayat. The Qur'an is miraculous by nature. Fateha should be enough for you. Why isn't Fateha enough for you? It has such genius that if you plumb the meaning, you will never get to the end of it.

I'm not suggesting that we shouldn't study the Qur'an, but there comes a point in your life when you want essences, you don't want a plethora. You don't want multiplicity; you want singularity. You want clean lines. When you start seeing the deen from that point of view, your practice is no longer a practice of working with content. It's working with intention, with essence.

Working with intention is the route out of basing your identity on your deen, toward using your deen to deconstruct your identity. It is because it becomes a means to escape yourself. The same sajda a year ago was me being a good Muslim among Muslims. Today, it is the very place where I bury my face in the sand. Why do I bury my face in the sand? Because I seek to disappear. Because my face is my identity and, when I put my face on the ground, I become a nobody. I seek not to appear. I seek to disappear.

This is the paradox that we are busy with on this path. We appear to be doing the same thing as everybody else but, in essence, exactly the opposite of that is happening. We're on a path which seeks to reintroduce us to our wildness, our essential identity, which is beyond what other people have made of us. When you see me from the outside, you see a man like any man: a citizen of the city, well-dressed like my companions, courteous and correct as I have been taught to be. But actually, strip off my clothes and I am constructed from the entire universe.

There is a quote from Rumi in this regard. 'Before I was a man, I was a mammal. Before I was a mammal, I was a lizard. Before I was a lizard, I was a fish. I have all within me. I am the walking macrocosm'.

To say I am Ebrahim with my clothes is a convenience so that I don't go crazy. In reality, we are far more - far, far greater than merely human. That's what this path tries to introduce us to - our essential nature, which is of the stars. It is beyond reckoning. It is that which Allah SWT proclaims when He says, 'I'm closer than your jugular vein'.

It is understandable that, historically, there's been a tension between the sincere people of tasawwuf and the orthodox. It is right that the tension should be there. In fact, it is immensely helpful to the people of tasawwuf that the tension should be there. It's good for you to be vilified. It's good for you that you're made insignificant. It's good for you to be made to be trash, to be considered despicable and destructive, and they want nothing to do with you. Who are you to be wanting to appear in the first place?

To deliberately pursue vilification is a perfectly legitimate path. We should thank those who vilify us because they are your helpers. We have no license to disapprove of them for it. We have only a command from our Rabb to be grateful to Him for it. They are providing the pressure or the gymnasium that forces us to grow.

The matter of the elite is the matter of intention. When you ride your Islamic identity as a vehicle, then you get delivered to the door of intention. The elite escape the tyranny of being socially compliant because, while they are stuck with the words or the nice forms, they actually want to find out what this really means. They pursue intention.

When they pursue intention, the elite get delivered to another door: the door of experience. You no longer assert that there is none but Him; you experience that there is none but Him. No matter how profound, your erudite description of honey is not the same thing as a mouthful of honey. These are different realities. So there's a point where you escape the whole issue of language and of meaning and of intention into the realm of direct experience — attention. That is the world of the elite of the elite. That is what we're aspiring to do.

When you occupy that place of experiencing this continuity, then you are unassailable, and you only need one sajda. Every sajda is the only sajda. It's not about multiplicity anymore. Only one aya is all that is needed, as it encompasses the entirety of the Qur'an. You only need a single salat because every salat is your last salat. You only need one embrace because every embrace is the last embrace. You are already dead.

Alhumdullilah.

May Allah SWT grant us nearness to Him,
May He grant us annihilation in Him,
May He grant us death before we die.

Chapter 19

UNLOCK YOUR LIFE
Discourse 19: 22 August 2019

Bismillah ar-rahman ar-raheem

There are two kinds of competencies fundamentally that a person builds a life on. The first competency is competency in action. This is about achieving things in the world. It is therefore concerned with being capable of changing things and affecting things in the world, in pursuit of one's own interests or agenda. It's about achieving outcomes. It's about being successful in the pursuit of goals.

The second competency is not concerned with action. It's concerned with perception. In this competency, what you achieve and what you do is not nearly as important as how you see and what you see. Bear in mind that when we say it's a competency in perception, it's obviously not just visual. It's all your perception.

The first competency is really concerned with changing the world to suit the self, whether that self is the individual or the collective. It is about engaging the outward, the world out there, to produce things that would be in the interest of and in the design of the self. The second competency is not about changing the world to suit the self. It's about shifting the self in such a way that it fits the world. In that sense, these competencies are not complementary. They are contradictory because their effect on the world is very different.

The first competency, which is about changing the world, has an implied judgement that the world isn't good enough. I have to fix it so that it suits me. The basic demeanour of the self that is competent in this way is one of negation and of judgement of others and of the world.

On the other hand, the person whose competency is competence in perception is one whose basic experience is that the world works by an ingenuity that is so extraordinary that, if you saw things as they are, you would recognize that seeing things as they are is good enough. In other words, if seeing things as they are isn't good enough for you, you're not seeing things as they are. You witness that your life works by an ingenuity which is so extraordinary, that has such fine balance to it, that all the things that you do in pursuit of your own happiness to make the world suit you are actually interfering with a design that is greater than you. Otherwise, why would it make sense to say:

wa makaru wa makarallahu wallahu khayr al-makireen

And they planned, but Allah planned. And Allah is the best of planners.

That implies that your plans and your plots, all the things you do to produce outcomes in your favour, are superseded by a higher intelligence which already has outcomes far in excess of your genius in store. And you can only witness that and experience that when you stop acting in your own interest.

This does not suggest that we should therefore not act. He can't demonstrate His genius until you have absolutely exhausted your own. This suggests that we have to engage this first competency to the point of destitution, to the point of absolute miserable, heart-rending, and tear-jerking failure, before we can sincerely recognize that our life works despite us.

It is in that moment of forgoing and giving up your plan that the real magic of being human happens. Which means you had to have had the plan in the first place. You had to have had the attempt to change the world. And you had to have had the engagement. What I found quite extraordinary in my life was the hunger, the brokenness, that sits behind every one of my actions. Why does anybody do anything? Why do you want to provide clothing? Why do you want to teach children? What sits underneath is a yearning, like an unrequited love. It is a brokenness that seeks to be healed.

This is such a subtle thing, that most of us are not aware that it's there. It produces a compulsive spirit to our actions. I am conscious that I'm going to do this or I'm going to do that, but I am unaware of the hunger that sits underneath. It's a vague shadow at the back of our attention.

On this path, commence by pursuing the thing that you want to the point of complete exhaustion, to the point where you've done everything, and you then recognize that this itch isn't getting scratched. That is when we truly give up. Then we see that He brings an outcome which is far bigger and better than ours. It is that outcome which will scratch the itch. At that point, you recognise that your whole life, with all of its needs and all of its little brokennesses, desires, and heartaches, is incredibly beautiful and has the most extraordinary design. It is like a lock, the key to which is not what you do; it is what you stop doing. And then you can die. Then your life has been requited. It fits. Our deep yearning is requited. It has clicked. That is fanaa. That's giving up, forgoing the illusion of existing as a separate being because, clearly, once it's clicked, it's one.

The second competency that I spoke of is a competency which is concerned with the development of perception - seeing that all is deeply well and has always been. That there is nothing out of place and all is well with your life. Your life works. So, in that sense, we will all come home. The alienation that we suffer from as human beings will be healed. That is why we say that if seeing things as they are is not good enough for you, you are not seeing things as they are. When you see things as they are, you are filled with such an overwhelming experience of gratitude that there's no emptiness left that needs to be filled. There's nothing that needs to be achieved over there. There isn't any hunger anymore. Your being is not an emptiness that needs to be sated. It is a fullness that overflows.

May Allah SWT grant us nearness to Him,
May He grant us annihilation in Him,
May He grant us death before we die.

Chapter 20

BEFRIENDING EXISTENCE
Discourse 20: 22 January 2010

Bismillah ar-rahman ar-raheem

We have two basic modalities that we exist in as human beings. The predominant modality for most people is that they function under the assumption that they exist separately from, and somehow contradistinct to, the world. The other modality is that you recognize that you are not separate from the world, that there's a oneness which connects you with all things. This second way of experience is indeed something to aspire to because a person who has reconnected their experience of life with the rest of existence has befriended existence. Whereas a person who experiences himself as being alive, separate from existence, has declared war on existence and has a basically hostile experience of life.

A person who experiences their life as separate from what is other than them is faced with the problem of being a very small being in a very threatening and very big universe. This is a being that has to look after itself. A small being under threat is a small being that seeks to protect itself, so at the root of this small being's experience is fear. That fear can be expressed as something very subtle, but it is still the groundwork of their day-to-day experience. It is that fear which creates the condition where this person needs to look after themselves. Their basic engagement with the world is one of taking.

Being here to take creates the conditions of weakness. As we have explained before, if you want something from somebody else, that person has power over you and the power that they have over you makes them dangerous to you. Also, precisely because you try to get something out of the other, you become dangerous to that person. So your relationship with the other is hostile. And because that relationship is hostile, it is fundamentally competitive. And a competitive relationship is one where two people cannot occupy the same space. They repel each other. They stay in irremediable conflict.

A being who knows that they are connected to the rest of the universe can afford to be generous with life because they realise that they are intimately connected with something far bigger than themselves. This bigger continuity has brought them to this point and is likely to look after them in the future. Their basic experience is one of trust, rather than fear. And because their basic experience is one of trust, they can afford to be generous with the world. This creates the conditions where they serve the other.

The other is safe from them, and they are safe from the other. And when two people are safe from each other, you have harmony. This means that the self that experiences that they are connected to the world fundamentally lives in a state of harmony with the world. This being can cohabit and can coexist in the same space with other people. This person is not competing.

This implies that the issue of living with and learning to live with is a core tool on the path of escaping the loneliness and the vulnerability of the illusion that you live as a separate being. Allah SWT has given us a massive gift, and that gift is other people and living with other people.

This experience of having a separate existence can be referred to as nafs, and it is manifest in any situation, in any experience, where you feel negated. There are so many ways in which we, as human beings, can convince ourselves that we have been negated or put down. When somebody says something to you that you take umbrage at, you are saying, 'You and I are not the same'. In organisational life, you see this very often where people start to have feuds around turf and roles. A person in one department gets upset with the person in another department because the person in the other department did something which was not part of their job description. We get rancorous about people invading our roles.

Even small things like another person's crankiness early in the morning can cause us to take exception, to feel insulted, demeaned, and take offense. We have innumerable ways of setting up our experience of other people such that we cannot tolerate being in the same space as them. These are all manifestations of nafs, all manifestations of our illusion that we exist as separate beings.

How can your leg and your foot not occupy a connected space? If your foot was severed from your leg, you would no longer have a foot. How can bits of your body not cohabit? So, in the same way that bits of your body are connected, you are deeply connected to the world around you and to the people around you. When you say that I can't cohabit with you, it's like your limbs declaring independence from each other. You'd be in a sorry state if your limbs declared independence.

Allah SWT has given us the proximity of other people to rub off our jagged edges. Our jagged edges are the assumptions that we have about who we are. Understand that death has no interest in who you think you are. When the grim reaper walks through the door, he will not have a hint of sympathy for your convenience. He comes for you, whether it suits you or not. You are not here to follow your own plan. You are here to be connected with a plan which is far bigger than yours. That plan is a plan which is cosmic in character.

The blessing of living with people is that it demands that you give up your idea of who you are, in the spirit of cooperating. This spirit of learning to cooperate with people, of living with people, is not an end in itself, but it's a necessary step on the way. However, do understand that you haven't graduated beyond this step if other people fiddling in your pie still freaks you out. You only have the license to leave the company of people when they no longer irritate you. While they are irritating you, you haven't got the license to leave because they haven't fulfilled their role for you. They haven't knocked your corners off; they haven't polished you smooth.

So our first experience and expression of connectedness is with other people. Allah SWT has made us in such an extraordinary way that, in order to be human, we have to have a sense of being exiled from Him. The infant has just recently come from Allah SWT, so he is connected. As the infant goes through the stages of childhood and particularly adolescence, he gets taught and experiences that he exists separately, that he has to compete with the world. That is why adolescents are so frightfully competitive.

But then Allah SWT's trick is to stack our hormones against us so that, before you know it, you have to satisfy these urges, which have you, quite literally, holding the baby. Now there's no question that you're just looking after yourself because you can't just look after yourself, you have to look after the children. You are now stuck in a context where you have to live with other people. You have to start to cooperate and no longer compete.

From the exile and alienation of adolescence, you get reintroduced to the sense of connectedness with people by having to live with people, by having to connect with people, by having to cooperate with people. This is, by definition, having your will put second for the interests of the group and for other people. You develop the skill of tolerating and mollifying. But you will also have a hankering to flee them because they're really just too frightfully irritating. There are residual bits of the adolescent sitting in your chest with his raised fist saying, 'I want my own life'.

Your initial connectedness with other people is the result of knowing you are too vulnerable on your own. As you get older, however, you start recognizing that you are the caregiver. The adolescent is still taken care of. The man in his forties is now responsible.

However, by the time you start hitting your late fifties, you start recognizing that you can't look after things. The thing starts to unravel. Some of the children die and the house gets invaded. You start to realize that no matter how hard you work, you are busy with a futile enterprise. That these people that you connected with are all going to die. We're all dying. The insight is that annihilation is the truth if it's only about other people. You start to look past other people.

Looking past other people creates the opportunity for you to recognize that you are not just connected to other people, you are connected to the whole of the universe. Just like I'm having a conversation with other people, I'm actually having a conversation with my Rabb. And, in a sense, He had veiled Himself from me in my relationship with other people. That veiling was incrementally stripped away until the people weren't there anymore, and the connectivity was always with Him.

So, there's no spirituality without adab. Adab, in the first instance, means being socially and transactionally correct with other people. This is the brilliance of the deen, and this is the brilliance of the tasawwuf that has come with the deen. It is the understanding of the significance of being transactionally correct as a social being, and that this is part of the path.

The Rasul (s.a.w.s.) was very disapproving of monasticism because society is the path. Being correct with other people in the world is the path. You do what is right with other people, you learn how to cooperate with other people, and you learn the patience that is necessary to be able to coexist with other people. This creates the condition for you to engage the most high. We recognize then that community, for all its annoyances, is a blessing from our Rabb. He has given us the pathway whereby we escape the loneliness of our inherent selfishness and narcissism, and are reintroduced back to our deep connectedness with Him.

We also recognize that it is precisely having to live with other people that develops the sabr or the patience, to act on the basis of what is required of us, rather than on the basis of what we want. Every time we do that, every time we act on the basis of what is required of us rather than what we want, we've escaped the prison of our exile a little bit more. We've chipped away at another piece of the façade of the nafs.

So, ask yourself in your daily reflections whether your fundamental demeanour with other people today has been competitive or cooperative. How easy was it for you to cohabit with them, literally cohabit and inhabit the same space? Or did you keep on wanting to flee? Did you keep on wanting to escape to your private room and your own agenda? How easy was it for people to be in your company? These things are connected. If people find it difficult to be in your company, it's because in some way you're pushing them away.

Was I really enchanted with the people around me or was I, in my heart, really judging them? Be very deliberate about your own internal dialogue. Be very deliberate about how you describe your engagement with other people and hunt for competitiveness in your own thinking. Reflect on it, find it, and root it out. Change its character. You will have it because every human being alive has a nafs. You will find this competitiveness. Hunt for it, find it, and, when you find it, work on it so that its nature changes from competition to cooperation. From negating and judgement, to curiosity, appreciation, and celebration.

May Allah SWT grant us nearness to Him,
May He grant us annihilation in Him,

May He grant us death before we die.

Chapter 21

INTENT: THE UNIVERSAL LANGUAGE OF SINCERITY
Discourse 21: 18 August 2012

Bismillah ar-rahman ar-raheem

Allah SWT describes the Qur'an as a furqaan or as a discernment. One way of understanding the discernment is that it distinguishes between what is false and what is real, between the fake and the actual.

Another way of distinguishing between the fake and the actual is to say it is the difference between how things are, and how things appear to be. For people who come into the deen, like many of us, this is a troublesome distinction because we see something in the deen which resonates with our hearts. But we are presented with a wall of Arabic language and culture.

Further to this, the community that we come into carries a conviction that this culture that we are engaging in is the reality; that it is the truth. We struggle with this because there is a part of us that understands that you can be duplicitous in any language. You can lie in any language. You can have a mouth full of Qur'an, and act insincerely. The language of intention, the language of sincerity, transcends the language of culture. You can be insincere in Arabic, and you can be sincere in English. You can be insincere in any context or language.

So the reality that we are after - this discernment - is about discovering what is for real. And what is for real is the language of intent. The language of intent does not respect cultural boundaries or barriers. It transcends cultural boundaries and barriers. The very insistence that this thing is about a specific culture, and acquiring a specific culture, is itself false. It is itself part of the illusion. It is missing the point.

How many people have come through the Zawia and have been of sound heart, and did not speak a single word of Arabic? On the other hand, how many people have we seen who have had a very good Islamic education but were unsound in their intention?

This presents us with a problem because we often end up being diverted with a sideshow. This problem of our relationship with existence, our relationship with our Rabb, and the clarification of our intent gets diverted and subverted into learning a new culture. The danger in that is that we may end up not engaging with the deen at all. Very often I find mature people of sound mind asking why they need to learn another culture to get to know their Rabb. I must admit, the logic is sound. But I do fear these people stand the risk of proverbially throwing the baby out with the bathwater. This would be a tragic error.

While we don't seek to become second-class Arabs, this form that came from the Rasul (s.a.w.s.) is breathtakingly beautiful and does not belong to a particular cultural context.

If you apply the form, not as a way of gaining a new identity, but as a way of literally slipping out from underneath your identity, the technology that the deen gives you is stunning beyond belief.

The essence of the matter is about the clarification of our intent, the issue of our sincerity, and truly and deeply knowing that our lives are produced by an intelligent Lord who is a genius, and whose plan is infinitely bigger than ourselves. It is not just to know that but to witness it first-hand. It means that almost any culture is irrelevant because what we are referring to is an experience, not a word or a description. Now, it is true to say that the form and the content are not the same thing. It is true to say that the word dog is not the reality of a dog. But how on earth do you begin to look for the dog or even yearn to see it if there isn't a word dog? So we can't be completely dismissive of culture.

Castaneda had a very clever device. He called it 'controlled folly'. He said all human beings suffer from an illusion that their actions are somehow important and matter. However, in the full scale of all that is, if this entire planet went up in a puff of smoke, the universe won't hiccup. We are staggeringly small. Our idea that our actions are significant, or that our actions somehow make us significant, doesn't square with reality.

Everything we do is inflated with an unjustifiable sense of self-importance. All human action, in the full scale of things, is folly. It is based on illusion.

What Castenada points out is that a person of spiritual aspiration recognises that their action is folly. But they engage in controlled folly. In other words, they do it anyhow, but they do it quite deliberately. Not that they think that what they are doing is immensely significant, but they do it in order to do it well. They know that the belief that you can act in order to produce your own good is folly because you can't do yourself any good. Allah SWT does your good. But if you act as if you can do yourself good, fully knowing that you can't do yourself good, that's controlled folly. It is doing what you are doing with absolute commitment, without taking it too seriously.

Now when you engage the deen with that point of view, it becomes absolutely magnificent because every single thing in all of our practices asks you to forgo the outcome to the Rabb. In that sense, it is controlled folly.

The last point that Castenada makes, which is very helpful in this context, is what's the discernment between ordinary folly and controlled folly? He says that the difference is that the controlled folly is the path of the heart. There is something very special that happens to you as you go into sajda, when you are doing it deliberately and consciously and your attention is on the musalla. It is truly heart-melting. It is truly beautiful.

That's why we do this. It is those little moments of childlike awe, experiencing the proximity of the Rabb. That's why we do all of this.

Otherwise, we are doing this because we think we can be of use to ourselves: I'm in sajda because I'm busy writing up an account in akhira, or I'm in sajda because my brothers will see me, and they will think I'm so pious. If you're doing any of the practices of the deen from that point of view, it is straightforward folly; it is no more useful to you than playing a Beetles song or arguing with your neighbour. What makes folly controlled folly is that, as you do it, you feel the proximity of the Rabb. You are no longer a doer; you are a witness and knower. A lover.

Our path is not a path of doing, it is a path of witnessing. We do in order to witness. We do in order to be perceivers and experiencers. The very specific experience that we are pursuing is the proximity of the Rabb, our beloved.

When you engage your deen from that point of view, there is no room for a sense of superiority: 'Oh, I am better than you because I wash my backside with water' or 'I am superior to you because I eat with my fingers, or wear my trousers above my ankles, or can recite this much Qur'an'.

As soon as there is this element of competitiveness and of judgement of others, then your deen is no longer a path of the heart. It is no longer something that you practice because, as you walk into the door, it becomes a garden of delight. It becomes a heavy thing. It becomes a thing of domination and of arrogance.

All of the cultural chauvinism that new Muslims experience from the traditional Muslim communities is because the traditional Muslim communities do not practice their deen in a way that is a garden of delight. They practice their deen as judgement and competition.

I appeal to Allah SWT to make it clear to me, and to all of us, what the distinction is between sincerity and fake, between reality and illusion, and to keep us with the reality.

I pray that Allah SWT enables us to use our deen as a tool to explore our intent and our sincerity, not as a tool to accumulate evidence of our superiority.

Chapter 22

WE ARE NOT NAFS, WE ARE RUH

Discourse 22: 17 December 2011

Bismillah ar-rahman ar-raheem

In the aya that Sidi Kamardine recited, Allah SWT reminds us that he made us from oneself. That means that it doesn't matter who you're speaking about or who you're speaking to, the essential nature of the human self is the same. Its genesis is in suffering. Not only is it the same, but its unfolding is exactly the same. The pattern whereby your nafs purifies and grows is the same for a person who is in China, as it is for an aboriginal person in Australia, as it is for South Africans. The same pattern. The same deep rules.

That pattern becomes apparent when you do an exercise like we did today. When each person just briefly describes their biography, what becomes apparent is that each one of us is dealing with similar themes. Beyond a certain number of people, it really wouldn't matter who is in the group and who is out of the group, the same pattern of themes comes to the fore.

The themes are just this: our nafs is concerned with our individual identity and what we think we want from life. Our nafs is based on our conditioning, all the things that have happened to us. That conditioning is a little bit like the tarnishing of a window. You can say that the window of perception that we described yesterday is not clear for most of us. Most of us don't see things as they are because our internal dialogue gets in the way. Our internal dialogue is quite literally like excretion, like dirt, on the window of perception.

This suggests that very often you're looking at your own muck rather than looking at the world. That muck is the accumulated elements of conditioning that have produced who you think you are. We call this being who you think you are the nafs. It is the principle whereby you assume that you are separate from the world. Allah SWT has made it to be the same for every human being alive.

Our path is from how we experience ourselves as individual beings, as separate beings, to being acquainted with our deepest and truest reality. And that is that we aren't nafs, we are ruh. At the depth of our being, there's a changeless, unconditioned, and unconditional root, which is our essential nature. This nature is belied by our sense of individual existence. Our path is about cleaning up the window, cleaning up our conditioning, so that increasingly we see things as they are. We decondition ourselves.

When we decondition ourselves, we incrementally, step-by-step, stop existing as individuals. Your sense of identity, your sense of who you are, is based on your conditioning. Your nafs is based on your conditioning - all the things that have happened to you produce a storyline of who you are. We keep that storyline alive as we walk through the world. We render comments on the world as we walk through it. Those comments don't say anything about the world; they say something about us. It is a recitation of what you consider significant, what you consider important.

In other words, you're constantly reinforcing your conditioning and, therefore, your conditional motive by the commentary you render on the world as you pass through it. The sum total of that pattern of conditioning can be called nafs. The basic principle of the conditioned self is that it sets itself apart from the world. This is true for every human being alive. All human beings have nafs and every nafs has the same architecture. It is a bundle of conditioning which then sets the perceiver apart from the world.

What is also true about this journey is that while we are concerned about holding onto our individual identity and what that requires from the world, we suffer. In fact, it is by His decree that we suffer. All the stories we heard bore the theme of forgoing outcomes in order to do what is appropriate in the moment that you're in. Sidi Ahmad had a story about his experience of finally walking away from politics. Siditi Azmat spoke about a baby and how it completely changes one's priorities and makes one focused.

What this suggests to me is that we're made from one nafs, and that nafs is defined in suffering the discontent of the world not being as we would want it to be. It's defined as a sense of separateness from the world and a sense, therefore, of being under threat. The escape from that nafs is Allah SWT's plan for us; the shift of how we operate from refracting our attention to operate from nafs to refracting our attention to operate from ruh. This is consistent with turning our intention from what we want to what Allah SWT wants.

The journey from constructing our motive from what we want to what Allah SWT wants is a preordained journey. He aims absolutely every intervention in every moment in our life in that direction. Every moment in your life has the same basic plot. You present the world with what your conditioning has convinced you that you want. He presents you with a situation that is utterly at odds with what you want and, moreover, wants something from you.

Basing your response on what is required of you, rather than what you want, is the incremental, step-by-step pathway out of your exile. Your sense of existing as an individual is based on your biography, which was accumulated step-by-step. It was laid up by increments over time. So other than killing yourself, which I don't recommend that you do, the way out of that must also be incremental. In this incremental stripping away of our suffering self, Allah SWT does eighty percent of the work. This is one of the significances of the idiom that says that if you take one step towards Allah SWT, he takes ten steps towards you.

What Allah SWT presents you with every day is as profound as the week that we've all just had. Every person here has said this week was one of the most significant of their lives. Do you think it was any different from last week, or the week prior to that, or five weeks ago? Of course, it wouldn't be. In fact, every week is profound. We're just too busy to recognize it.

Every week has these little cameos like the beautiful cameo of what happened to Sidi Adil with the two sparrows. You'll remember he said that he was driving, and he saw this wounded sparrow in the face of oncoming traffic being rescued by another sparrow, who picked it up and flew with it to the top of the traffic light. Subhanallah. What an affirmation that life looks after its own. That al-hayy, the living, looks after its own.

When you've allied yourself with that, you don't need a plan. From some completely unpredictable corner, a little sparrow will come to save you. While the monster machine is trundling down on you, followed by bankers and debt and all the frightening things that our modern world can aim at you, there is a miracle waiting for you.

Allah SWT gives us these little vignettes. In every moment, in every situation, there's a little cameo if you would only see it. If you look out for it, every single day will be peppered with these sparrow events. However, we mostly don't see them because we're too busy pursuing our own agenda.

So the first bad news about escaping the suffering of existing as an individual - escaping operating from nafs - is that it's a step-by-step thing. It's not going to happen instantaneously. When it happens instantaneously, you will have a dysfunctional person on your hands because no one can come from the depth of darkness into unrelenting light without being burned. We have to get there in little steps. So pray that it doesn't happen instantaneously. Pray that it happens by increment.

However, those increments can be quite fast, depending on what you bring to the party. This is borne out by a metaphor that we've repeated a number of times here. Allah SWT is having a discourse with us. We know that wherever you turn you see the face of Allah SWT. And what does a face do? A face speaks. So wherever you look, Allah SWT's face is saying something to you. He uses events as words and time as grammar. There is an unfolding meaning that's happening on an ongoing basis.

This suggests that His speech is not only the Qur'an. His speech is also the world that faces you and every moment is another aya, another revelation to you. The purpose of this revelation is to enable you to take the next step closer to home from exile. Another way of seeing this conversation that you are having with Him is that it is both a love letter and a treasure map. The key register of a love letter is enchantment, infatuation, and love.

As nafs, we think of ourselves as small beings that have to battle it out against the world which, in essence, produces a narrative of self-pity. Life is tough. But if you reflected for a moment on what it has taken to produce you, the millennia of events that have had to happen since the first moment to produce the conditions for your life, how can you doubt that you are the most beloved of all existence? The whole of the universe colludes to make you possible.

The other, the face that Allah SWT gives you, has you as its object. It is saying to you, 'My beloved, my beloved, my beloved, my beloved'. This conversation that you're having with your Rabb is a conversation of love. If this were not the case, you would be dead. Your Rabb is the most powerful. If He did not consider you worthy of being here, do you think you'd be here? If He did not love you, if He did not consider you a worthy focus of all of existence, you would be dead.

The second character of this conversation that you have with your Rabb is that this speech that is coming to you from Him is also a treasure map. Treasure maps say, 'You're now at point A. You have to take ten steps north and then you'll be at point B. And then you have to turn left at 3 degrees. And then you have to take another 15 steps to the rock that is green' and so on. It defines, moment by moment, what you should do.

This is also how we escape from suffering. Your Rabb says to you, 'At this moment, this is what you want, this is what your nafs wants, and this is what your conditional motive is. However, this is what I require from you. Do this specific thing and you will take the next step toward the treasure'.

In other words, what He is saying to you is this is what you want to get, and this is what I want you to give. This is the contribution that you should be making in this situation. If you act in the situation on the basis of what you want to get, if you act on the basis of your nafs, you will stay at that spot. You will not progress. Over time, that spot becomes more and more intolerable, to the point where it becomes so intolerable, and you shift your intent to what He wants from you.

When you shift your intent in the moment from what you want to what your Rabb wants from you, when you act appropriately, you graduate from the position that you're in, to the next step on the treasure map. You become closer and closer to the prize of prizes. What is the prize of prizes? The prize of prizes is baqaa'. It is going on. Then you have ceased to operate as an individual being. Your nafs no longer defines who you are. It has been annihilated. Alhumdullilah. It has been smashed. And what you discover is the continuity that sits underneath this is ruh.

In the second surah that Sidi Kamardine recited, Allah SWT reminds us that He made us from a clot of blood. He continues by saying anything is possible; He just commands a thing, and it is. He has created you from a thing which human beings consider to be polluted and despicable. From that, He has made you who you are. Do you not think that it is possible for Him to rescue you from your suffering? Do you not think that it is possible for Him to rescue you by kun fa yakuun?

Any step on the treasure map could be the last step. That last step may appear to be a very insignificant thing. You're sitting at the restaurant, you've just ordered a coffee, and the waitress delivers the coffee. You could ignore the woman, or you could look at her and say, 'Thank you very much'. It may be that that appropriate act is the one that hits just the right angle. In that moment, you are a trainwreck, bewildered beyond belief. Suddenly, going back to Sidi Abdi's experience, you've shrunk to the point of disappearance, and you've discovered who you are. You are not the small one; you are the magnificence that encapsulates it all.

Every moment has that potential by your Rabb's decree and it's not necessarily the dramatic thing. It's not necessarily the heroic storming across the field in the face of machine gun fire. It could be the last sajda of two rakaats done, almost on a whim, under the stairs one night because you couldn't sleep. It could be the courtesy to allow somebody in the traffic through.

The miraculous is in the small things. It's not in the big things. This path is about learning to be really careful with the small things. Sidi Ahmad spoke of forgoing a political agenda to help the drunk on the corner who would otherwise be mugged. It's those small things that matter. Every moment has within it a price that your Rabb is asking of you. And any one of those moments could be the bonus, the billion-dollar prize, the escape. So this is why, on this path, we are cautioned to be vigilant. We watch moment by moment like a hawk. We do not allow ourselves this distraction, this being caught up in our internal dialogue. Because the more we do that, the more we cycle. We miss the treasure, the prize of prizes, which is to discover that the other is encapsulated by the totality of the self. You are the vessel that contains the entire universe.

Alhumdullilah.

May Allah SWT grant us nearness to Him,
May He grant us annihilation in Him,
May He grant us death before we die.

Chapter 23

THE REALITY CONTAINED IN YOUR HEART
Discourse 23: December 2011

Bismillah ar-rahman ar-raheem

In one of the ayat which Imam recited, Allah SWT reminds us 'inna lillahi wa inna ilayhi raji'uun', which means: Verily, we come from Allah and we will return to Allah'. This means that, amongst other things, our essence or our fundamental nature is from Him. It is that which will endure, that's what will go back to Him.

We're also told that the entire universe can't contain Allah SWT, but the heart of a mu'min can contain Allah SWT. In other words, there is a way of being, which is about being a sincere believer, that contains the whole of existence. We just described this phenomenon before dhikr, by describing the difference between the person who is in the world and the person who realizes that the world is in them.

The person who realizes that the world is in them is the person who we can describe as containing the reality in their heart. Allah SWT is outwardly manifest. Wherever your eye goes, wherever you look, is the face of Allah SWT. If you contain that, then Allah SWT is within you. So there is a way of being where you, the apparently small one, can be the vessel which contains the source of it all.

Further, that is your fundamental reality, your fundamental truth. The truth that you've come from and the truth that you're going to go back to is that you are the one who encapsulates all existence. You are not in the world; the world is in you. The self is not encapsulated by the totality of the other, but the other is encapsulated by the totality of the self. That is the truth.

Your experience that you are the small one surrounded by a vast universe which has you under threat - under the threat of extinction - is an illusion. It has to be an illusion if your Rabb tells you that you've come from Me and you're coming back to Me. You've come from Me, the eternal, the transcendent, the ineffable, the all-wise, the all-knowing. That's where you've come from. And you're going back to that. So how can you be under threat? How can you be the small one? How can you be the one who is defenceless in the face of the vastness?

Our outer reality is our apparent reality because outwardness is about appearance and how things are seen to be. This apparent reality is that we are small. If I look at Sidi Harun next to everything that isn't Sidi Harun, I'd say that he is rather a pitiful creature because he is under threat. There is a big universe out there, half of which is filled with predators that would like to feast on your flexitarian flesh. So the outward appearance is that we are small and under threat. The inward reality is that we are vast beyond description.

How is it then that we experience ourselves to be small and under threat? It has to be because, at some level, we have decided to vote for appearance rather than reality. We have cast our lot with the illusion and the shadow show rather than the haqq and the truth. We have taken how things appear immensely seriously. So staggeringly seriously that we honestly believe that you can judge the man by his clothes; that the wisdom of the Shaykh has got something to do with the number of turns in his turban.

While we hook our aspiration onto how we appear, we stay the small one under threat. We are dealing with the world in the realm of the outward. And outwardly, yes, you are the small one under threat. The truth of your being, that you are the vessel of wakefulness that contains the entire universe, is hidden. It's not apparent. That is your secret truth, your inner truth. It's not your outer truth.

So if you want to taste that reality, you have to aspire to a different arena. Most of us desire to have the wealth of the world through the accumulation of possessions. We study to accumulate knowledge, we work to accumulate assets, and we commit to our profession to accumulate acclaim. These are all about achievements in outer things. They're not necessarily bad achievements and they're not necessarily selfish achievements. Maybe it's about providing for the family, or putting a roof over your head, or having a secure future, or having an enjoyable career, or becoming a significant person; they're all about outward appearances.

How do you propose to escape the tyranny of the apparent for the security of the real if you don't dedicate a significant amount of aspiration and work to inner achievement? It's naïve. The starting point of that work is five prayers a day.

However, that is not sufficient. Allah SWT Himself indicates that nearness to Him doesn't just come from the five prayers. Nearness to Him comes from supererogatory acts. In other words, the extra work or the further work. It is as if the basics are just basic hygiene. It's about staying safe. But there's something more than basic hygiene that's required. If you want to achieve in the realm that matters – the inner realm, the realm of the reality of your being where your true power lies – don't think that it's just going to happen. You have to take active pursuit of it.

Another thing that Sidi Kamardine recited from our Rabb is that He is with those who are patient. Those who are patient are those who forego their outer aspiration. The model of patience is, 'Johnny, you can't have the ice-cream now. You first have to finish your studies. Or you first have to eat your peas'. Patience is about the ability to forego outcomes. It is about the ability to suspend your own gratification or the thing that you want to get. How do you propose to pursue your inner truth if you aren't willing to be patient with your outer aspiration? If you're unwilling to forego your outer aspirations by leaving them with Him?

You see, the reason why He is with those who are patient, those who persevere patiently, those who forego outcomes and hand them to their Rabb, is because those are the ones who give themselves a slight possibility of discovering what their true natures are. It makes it possible for them to discover that their true nature is nothing other than Allah SWT. Know yourself and you'll know your Rabb. Now, go into the depths of where your perception operates from, on the inside, and you'll find Him. You'll find the vessel that contains the universe. This is our secret reality. This is our secret truth.

Outwardly, you'll always remain the puny one. It's not possible for it to be otherwise; outwardly, you will become old, you will lose your teeth, you will lose your eyesight, you'll find you need a stick, and you'll die. Outwardly you are under threat; outwardly you are always compromised. You're a catastrophe waiting to happen. Shaykh Abdul Qadir used to say that we're in this breathtaking rush to death. That's your outward truth.

Your inner truth is that the apparent rush to annihilation is, in fact, the rush to go on. Inna lillahi wa inna ilayhi raji'uun. This vastness, which is your true nature, that's who you're going to. So nothing is threatening you. Death is not a threat to you. Death is only a threat to you when you settle for appearances, when you settle for the outward.

If you make your aspiration to discover what your true nature is, and you pursue that and work at that, then death very quickly becomes your ally, not your enemy. It becomes the one that's anticipated joyfully, not the one that's viewed with horror and apprehension.

May Allah SWT grant us nearness to Him,
May He grant us annihilation in Him,
May He grant us death before we die.

Chapter 24

PURSUING THE DIVINE ENCOUNTER
Discourse 24: 12 January 2013

B ismillah ar-rahman ar-raheem

This evening is the coming together of old friends, a reconnecting of hearts, and so it occurs to me that it would be appropriate to explore and remind myself of the key assumptions of our path and of this endeavour that we're busy with here.

This endeavour is about the divine encounter. It is possible to have an experience of arrival or of connectedness with the Rabb which, in the deepest sense, transcends all your insecurity. Which provides, at a stroke, an experience of fulfilment, of harmony with the world around you, and a deep sense of power. In short, it is possible to experience the fruit of the highest of your aspirations, which is to disappear into the folds of the Rabb.

In saying that, we commence by reminding ourselves that this experience is unusual. This experience of the divine encounter is foreign for most people; even glimpses of it are foreign for most people. In that sense, He is a hidden treasure to most people. What is peculiar about this hidden treasure is that this hidden treasure is very proximate. He says of Himself that He is closer to us than our jugular vein. He is not distant; He is proximate. It is like we're sitting on the treasure, but it has been hidden from us in the most extraordinary way because it is immediately apparent and obvious, and yet we don't see it.

Allah SWT's plot with the creation of all things was that He was a hidden treasure that sought to be known. How does that which is hidden, which seeks to be known, become known other than by being rediscovered? For it to be rediscovered, it suggests that it was once not covered, but became covered so that it can be rediscovered.

As infants, we come fresh from the presence of the Rabb. Infants are deeply connected to the divine presence. But as they grow up and as we socialise them, we cauterise them. We increasingly restrict that access so that they become useful people. They lose that sense of connectedness. It becomes hidden until, at the time of adulthood, they pursue this path, or a path similar to this, which is about rediscovering that nature. In rediscovering that nature, there are two endeavours and they are mutually enabling, like one hand washes the other. There's an inward endeavour and there's an outward endeavour.

The inward endeavour is about deconditioning your experience and your intention. The simplest way of describing that is that it is about forgoing what you want and committing to what Allah SWT wants. The very structure of how He becomes hidden from us is that we assume that what makes us happy is elsewhere - it's in the future, it's on the other side of a transaction. It is, 'I have to do this in order to get that'. But He's proximate. He's not on the other side. He's not at the arrival point of the transaction; He is in the process of the transaction.

It is as if we're looking over the garden wall for something that's lying in front of the garden wall. There's a process to this of learning how to look again - learning to see that which is in front of the garden wall, that which is proximate. That process of learning to see that which is in front of the garden wall is about forgoing the endeavour of looking over the wall.

Looking over the wall is looking for that which is over there: the wealth that is going to make me happy, the woman who is going to make me happy, the car that is going to make me happy, or whatever. It's not over there, it's over here.

All the practices that we do - the dhikr, the salat – have the same effect, which is to silence you for a moment. It shuts you up on the inside. And that silencing allows you to experience that which is lying in front of the wall, that which is near to you, that which is proximate: His presence. While you're experiencing that, you have a sense of deep contentment. But then your mind starts going again and you start looking beyond: 'That's going to make me happy' or 'This is going to make me happy'.

What's also true about this process of becoming quiet on the inside is that we become skilled at it by increments. It is a step-by-step process. Sometimes a person goes into the khalwa for the first time and comes out after two days feeling disappointed because he didn't see a flash of lightning and the heavens didn't open. But this is a patient thing. It takes years of endeavour.

If you truly managed to create the condition where you sat without thinking for an hour, you would have an hour in the divine presence. There's no question about it. The only thing that separates you from the divine presence is your internal dialogue.

What's also important about this becoming quiet on the inside is that it is also about reengineering and changing your intention. Your sense of being an isolated being is simultaneously defined as your intent to get stuff from the world. The moment you deal with the other on the basis of wanting something from them, you're saying 'I'm in-self-sufficient', 'I am compromised', or 'I am needy'. Your intent to take confirms your boundaries, your inadequacy, and your weakness. It confirms the fact that you and the other are the opposite.

If you want something from somebody else, you are creating a schism between you and them. The moment you act on the basis of what is in their best interest, you are transcending the difference between you and them. Which means that this escape from our exile is not just about working on the inside because it has to be reflected in intention. And it is the intention to serve that connects you with the world. It's when your body says the interests of the other and the self are not opposite, they are the same.

I then experience that I exist as connected to everything around me. I don't exist as opposite to everything that's around me. It is not just good enough to do inner work. This inner work has to be reflected in transactions. Just like the inner work is about an incremental quietening down or derailing of all of your conditional motives, the outer work is about an incremental forgoing what you want. It is about increasingly being able to, radically and absolutely, do what Allah SWT wants from you in the situation, rather than to act on the basis of what you want in the situation.

At the beginning of the path, it is not only important to commit to daily practice, the daily quieting of your internal dialogue, and examining what goes on inside your soul so that you can understand how your intention works. This transacting in order to contribute starts off with the intent not to harm.

Before the intent to do good is the intent not to do bad. Doing good is transacting in such a way that the other is enriched by your transaction. The beginning of doing good is transacting in such a way that the other is not harmed by your transaction. So it is to refrain from any transaction where you get something for nothing. This is the significance of riba. The significance of riba isn't just interest; it is that you refrain from transactions in which you get something for nothing.

That graduates into transactions that are deliberately constructed on the basis of the best interest of the other. In other words, they are constructed not only not to harm the other, but to further the other. That is what your Rabb wants from you. Start off by just not harming them, and then serve them.

Incrementally acting, increasingly and unconditionally, on the basis of the best interest of the other fixes the change in your consciousness. This journey of the deconditioning of yourself is about deconditioning your motive.

One of the significances of the idiom 'the road to hell is paved with good intentions' is that people intend to do good, but they do bad. The intent to do good means absolutely nothing if you aren't doing good. So it is not adequate just to intend to do good, you must act consistently with it. It is the action that fixes the change in your consciousness.

If, as a kid, you worked with fiberglass and resin, you would have noticed that the resin is a liquid. However, once you drip a tiny amount of catalyst into the resin, it becomes fixed, it sets, and you have a solid object. Before that, you had goo.

Your intention is the same – it stays goo until you add a drop of amilu saalihaat, or a drop of the appropriate action. And it's that action which galvanises the change of your consciousness. You could tell yourself as much as you like how connected you are with the world, how you are one with everything, and in what a blissful state you subsist. You can also announce to everyone else how benign you are, and even announce to yourself how benign you are. If that claim is not actually reflected in what you do, then that is the road that has been paved to hell on good intentions.

This path means nothing if it doesn't affect how you act. You will not escape your exile if you don't act in such a way where your cells profess that you know that your highest interest lies in acting and serving the best interest of the other in every situation that you're in. That is what your Rabb wants from you. He says, 'How do I know that you trust that I exist? How do you demonstrate to Me that I am not a hidden secret from you, that I am an explicit reality for you?'. You act in a way that is apparently stupid. You act on the basis of the interest of anything other than yourself.

In every moment, He says to you, 'I've put in front of you a drama, so that you can act on the basis of what's right for the other'. That doesn't mean you're always sweet. Sometimes you can be very confrontative, but you act on the basis of what's right for the other. He says to you, 'I know you trust Me. I am your Rabb and now I can visit on you an inner experience of connectedness rather than hostility'.

We mostly experience hostility. The average person has a miserable experience of being inside their own skin. They wake up alienated and frightened and they go to bed alienated and frightened. They are stuck in the cycle of being alienated and frightened. But we are on a path which claims to be a straight path. It doesn't cycle. It leads it us out of the morass of suffering. It introduces us to the original nature that we had, which He lost for us so that we could find it.

May Allah SWT grant us nearness to Him,
May Allah SWT grant us annihilation in Him,
May He grant us death before we die.

Chapter 25

EMPTYING
Discourse 25: 15 September 2018

Bismillah ar-rahman ar-raheem

Tonight was indeed a very special night. Tonight we did the dhikr. You did it with commitment. You did not hold back. You did it in the spirit of emptying yourself of yourself. That's how one does this dhikr – you do it in the spirit of a complete disclosure of your being, of a complete opening up of your chest, knowing full well that you will not and cannot stand up to scrutiny. Because none of us can. Knowing full well that your being is a web of duplicity, deceit, and self-deceit.

In our normal day-to-day lives, we play games upon games of wanting to make sure that we don't offend, make sure that we tread well and tread properly, and, in the process, we mince our way through our lives to the point where we don't have our lives. We mince ourselves out of our lives.

This night, the night of dhikr, is where we know our Rabb will embrace us irrespective of our duplicity, irrespective of our inauthenticity, irrespective of the deceit in our lives. For no other reason than that He loves us breathtakingly. He loves us to a degree that makes the love of a mother for a newborn infant paltry. He loves you to such an extent that every single minute metabolic detail that happens moment by moment to keep you alive is a result of Him commanding kun fa yakuun: be and it is. If you are in the hands of such a generous Rabb, who makes it all happen for you irrespective of your game-playing and your deceit, we can afford to be as we were tonight in His Presence. We can afford to be in His Presence naked - no restraint, no holding back, no playing a game, no worrying about what that one across the room thinks.

It is that single thought of 'What will they think?' which robs us of our ecstasy, which robs us of the heart-aching beautiful truth of our being.

It is this claim of self-sufficiency, of being unassailable, of having whole hearts, which is, in fact, our death trap. The only useful heart is a broken heart. The only useful heart is a heart that has been crushed like grapes. You have to crush the grapes for the wine and the juice to release their flavours. The sweetness of a man comes out when his heart is broken. Any man who has not had a broken heart, who doesn't consistently have his heart broken, is a man you can suspect of the disease of self-sufficiency and a lack of compassion. How can the one who has not had his heart broken have compassion for any other?

This dhikr is for the breaking of hearts. This dhikr is for the release of constraint. This dhikr is for the abandonment of the illusion that we are in any way self-sufficient. We are completely, nakedly, absolutely given up to Allah SWT. This dhikr is a celebration of that truth. I'm honoured to be among brothers who could demonstrate in this dhikr tonight that they have that taste, that they know that reality.

I pray that my Rabb keeps me in your company for a very long time. And that he keeps us growing in depth on this extraordinary mystery which is unfolding here, which is not the mystery of the successful. It is not the mystery of the whole ones and the healthy ones and the sane ones. It is the mystery of the broken and bereft. It is the mystery of those who are heartbroken. It is the mystery of those who are beyond redemption and at a complete loss.

May Allah SWT grant us nearness to Him,
May Allah SWT grant us annihilation in Him,
May He grant us death before we die.

Chapter 26

CAPTURING THE EXPERIENCE
Discourse 26: 23 January 2016

Bismillah ar-rahman ar-raheem

There's a saying from Neuro Linguistic Programming (NLP) that is very useful, which says the map is not the territory. If we had a large map of Pakistan on the carpet and there was a point on that map that said 'Lahore' and one of us stood on that point, you would not be in Lahore. You would be in a representation of Lahore. It's entirely feasible that you could have the knowledge of a cartographer and know the particular map really well, and not have a clue what a day in Lahore is like. Similarly, and you've heard this before, a man can write a dissertation about the taste of honey, the chemical components of its sweetness, and the effect of its sweetness on the human digestive tract, the tongue, and the taste organs, and yet not know the taste of honey because he has not had a single spoonful.

This is not to say that there isn't a place for learned discourses about honey, or there isn't a place for cartographers. Obviously, there's a place for these things. However, the endeavour that we're busy with here is the endeavour of first-hand experience. It's the endeavour of the taste of the honey and of actually going to the city of Lahore. To achieve that end, we have to do something quite risqué and challenging. We have to allow ourselves to pursue the divine encounter and the first-hand experience of the proximity of Allah SWT beyond the nomenclature and the words that we've been taught. It stands to reason that, just a man can know a lot about honey without having tasted it, so too can a man know a lot and recite a lot about the experience. But he cannot actually give his own account because he's not had it.

So, the endeavour that we're busy with here, the endeavour that this place is dedicated to, is in a sense a profoundly revolutionary one. Revolutionary in the sense of a rebellious one. It is one where we are willing to overthrow the paraphernalia in order to find the experience, to find the essence.

Having been involved in this endeavour for many years, my experience is that many people who are highly steeped in the nomenclature of tasawwuf actually have to overthrow the language and be forced to recast their understanding in ordinary plain English - in their own language - to have a taste of the real. If this is not done, what they have is the regurgitated, semi-digested nonsense from somebody else. It is not based on their own first-hand experience.

This task is of finding the jewel that is beyond the description. It doesn't matter how profound the language is, even if it is Arabic, it cannot capture the experience - that jewel which Allah SWT wants to give to you. The experience is based on a discovery. And, in the nature of all discoveries, that which is discovered is surprising and new. It is not old. The experience is a product of your own journeying. It is the outcome of finding out how your own attention works, how your life works, and how your relationship with people works. At the time when you first see it, it is so surprising that the language you had to describe it before will be wholly inadequate.

Shaykh Abu Madyan was famous for repeating to his mureeds, 'Bring me fresh meat'. What he meant by this is don't bring me stuff that other people have chewed, digested, and spat out. What is your unique insight? What is your unique experience? Allah SWT reveals Himself to each one of us in a completely unique way. Otherwise, your individuality would not have a purpose. So what is your unique contribution to the treasure trove of experience?

You've got two responsibilities here. The first responsibility is to find the treasure, to find the experience that He's made you uniquely to experience. You. The second thing is that you give voice to that experience. Because once you've discovered the uniqueness which is the jewel in the centre of your being and you give voice to it, that voice will have the ring of authenticity. It will be convincing. When people hear you, they say, 'Ah, but that's it. That's the truth'. Not the truth because they've heard the same thing recited a hundred times from somebody else or it comes out of a text. But because what comes out of your mouth is like living water.

So, if we consider His command to us in Surat al As'r:

illaladhina aamanuu wa-'amil-us-saalihati

those who believe and do what is correct

wa tawasaw bil-haqqi wa tawasaw bi-s-sabr

and enjoin one another to the truth and enjoin one another to patience

So, the first instance refers to those who have the experience and act accordingly. They see the truth of the extraordinary reality – that all of us are participating in the divine nature – and they act accordingly. And they bear witness to that truth to others. It's not just the experience alone that we are called to, but we're also called to bear witness to the experience. However, we first have to capture the experience. And I'm afraid that, for most of us, this has to actually amount to a book burning of a kind.

There's a reason why, when you get locked up in khalwa, you're not permitted to take any text with you. Why? This is because you're trying to find the experience, and text will just get in the way. By definition, the experience is so vast that you cannot capture it in words. It strikes you dumb. There's an unlearning that has to happen first. There's a stripping away that has to happen first.

A lot of the things that we have learnt have formed accretion on top of the experience because we've put our own youthful interpretation on the terms, even if they've been well-explained to us. If you ask, "What's a dog?", the reply may be that a dog is a four-legged predator. The words have created more words. Well, what's a four-legged predator? It's then described further. So, there's a circularity to it. It stays in the realm of language until you've been bitten by a dog. Then you realize 'Ah, that's a dog'.

May we all be bitten so that the next time we describe a dog, there's a sense of conviction that comes out of us. This person knows what they're talking about. This is not just words that beget more words, erudition that begets more erudition. This is a real experience. Very often, you can sit in the presence of somebody without them saying a word, and you know that they know. You see it in the glance of an eye. You see it in their posture. You even see it in the person's handshake. You see it in how they drink their tea.

The reality that we're after is essentially transmissive. It goes from heart to heart. And the essence of that transmission is not just an insight. It's the experience of safety, it's the experience that the ally is real, that He exists, that He has made you the beloved of existence. This is not speculative. You experience it like you experience the warm embrace of the person you love most.

May Allah SWT grant us nearness to Him,
May Allah SWT grant us annihilation in Him,
May Allah SWT grant us death before we die.

Chapter 27

IN DEFENCE OF AUTONOMY
Discourse 27: 16 October 2022

Bismillah ar-rahman ar-raheem

This week, a number of people have approached me who were clearly suffering. The question that was at the root of their suffering is, 'What is the point of all this? What is the meaning of all this? Why?' I think the 'why' is quite apparent. I think it's almost ridiculously easy, from one point of view, to figure it out. One does not need to be particularly intelligent. The problem is that the why for you being alive is not something that is necessarily going to make you useful to other people or successful in the world that we're in, because it's completely a function of being an awake and alive human being. That alone is good enough. That accounts for why you are here.

We get the sense that we've come into this world from another place, that we are foreigners here, that we're strangers here. This can't be true. There is nothing that you are made up of that doesn't come from this world. You are a product of this world. Your bones are constructed by minerals that come from the world. The blood that courses through your veins is in a matrix of water which you have drunk from the world. You are a product of the world, but you're a very peculiar product. You are a part of the world that is able to look back at existence. And when you look back at existence, the first thing that strikes you is a sense of scale. This place that you're looking at is really very big and you are not very big at all. So you are a part of existence that can look back on existence and apprehend scale. That apprehension of scale can produce one of two effects on you. You are either terrified by it all or you are enchanted by it. You are in awe of it. You recognize the design in it, you recognize the beauty of it, and you recognize the scope of it.

When you apprehend it as terrifying and overwhelming, you can only respond in the spirit of resistance because the consequence of that which overwhelms is to annihilate. You will be in terror of being annihilated. You will seek to control; you will respond in a spirit of distrust and suspicion. You will seek to fight back or hide – fight or flight.

On the other hand, you can respond in a spirit of love, of being enchanted with the world, amazed at it, in love with it. An analogue to this is that your response is informed by wanting to, out of love, or your response is a response of having to, out of fear. There are only two ways of being alive: one is an expression of love and the other is an expression of fear.

The possibility of Allah SWT being known, which is why He made us, has to be from a place that is not what He is. You can only truly apprehend the great if you are small. You can truly only truly apprehend the significant if you are insignificant. You are on the small end of the continuum that has the great on the other end. You are there so that you can be in love with that. In awe of that. Paradoxically, the response can only be one of awe if you have the autonomy to choose terror. If your love and awe were compelled from you, your response would not be of love or want to. It would be of terror or have to.

In other words, you have to choose awe. You have to choose love. This small thing called a human being looks at that which is out there, which is vast, and it has a choice. When it chooses love, it is saying to the rest of existence, 'You are magnificent. You are an expression of ar-rahman ar-raheem. You are the overflowing. You are effulgent. You are that which is wonderful'.

You can also say, 'You are terror. You are horror'. Both the awe and horror are possible, but the awe must be chosen. An example of this is the charge to children that they must love their parents. When I love to do something, I want to do it. When I have to do something that I don't want to do, I am compelled to do it. To think that you can compel a child to love their parent is to think loving and being in terror are the same thing. That is clearly false. Is love consistent with have to or is love consistent with want to? Is love consistent with autonomy or is love consistent with compulsion? Clearly, it is consistent with autonomy.

So you can't say to somebody, 'You must love'. Must love is about subjugation, it's about terror. We are Muslims. We are people of submission. Submission and subjugation are not the same. Submission is chosen. Subjugation is compelled. We have to have the freedom to choose awe because, if we don't choose awe, if our worshipfulness is forced out of us, that worshipfulness is no longer an expression of awe. It is an expression of fear.

Allah SWT has spent all of time creating these incredibly intricate conditions to make the possibility of the autonomous will, the independent will of the human being, possible so that human beings can choose awe. The pinnacle of creation is the autonomous human will. There is nothing higher because it is only the autonomous will that can choose love, that can choose awe. A will that isn't autonomous only acts out of fear.

Once one understands this, you have a key to look at the world around you with a reasonably incisive eye. You can see, for instance, how much of the world that you are in is actually about compulsion. Look at how people consider the deen. How much of what we consider being the deen today – orthodox expressions of the deen – are concerned with compulsion?

The Salafi phenomenon is a case in point. What's happening in Afghanistan and Iran seems to imply that to be Muslim is to be one who forces people into particular dress codes, particular behaviours, and, more peculiarly, particular beliefs. I thought – the word Islam means submission, and surely there's a difference between submission and subjugation. When your deen has become a means whereby you subjugate people, whereby you oppress them, whereby you rob them of the autonomy of their will, then surely your deen is no longer doing what it's supposed to.

Your deen is supposed to be making you worshipful and helping others to be worshipful. How can people be worshipful if their worship is compelled by them? That's not worship, that is terror. This peculiar propensity that we have of judging others, of thinking we are superior, of wagging fingers at others like this is a great competition, is unbecoming. We should be the ones who look out at the world in the spirit of awe, like the one who realizes how precious his own autonomy is. This person would be very careful to judge others.

Judgement is about putting people in boxes. It is about domination, about who's better. It's about putting people under the heel and under the thumb. We can't be people who are putting people under the heel and under the thumb. We have to be people of curiosity and kindness, not judgement and superiority.

I pray that Allah SWT is going to make something possible going into this next century. I pray He makes an opening for us as a species, where we truly get to prize the autonomy of the human. And where we enable the autonomy of the human to make it possible for the human to do what a human being should be doing, which is to be worshipful.

May Allah SWT grant us nearness to Him,
May He grant us annihilation in Him,
May He grant us death before we die.

Chapter 28

SEPARATION AND CONNECTEDNESS

Discourse 28: 27 October 2020

Bismillah ar-rahman ar-raheem

I'd like to pick up a theme that was raised by Sidi Ali Anwar from Islamabad. He referred to an experience of sadness, which he finds sitting as a backdrop to his being. I think this experience is very common, so common I suspect it is universally true. It is what Maulana Rumi referred to when he described the sound of the ney being played as the weeping or the longing of the reed for the reed bed.

Anything that exists has to stand out from that which it has come from. It gets cut off. This produces a feeling of melancholy which the Afrikaans author of the 1930s, Eugene Marais, described in his observation of baboons. Marais was a very keen naturalist, and his observation of baboons convinced him that they have the same experience as people, which becomes apparent at sunset and at sunrise. He said if you looked at the baboons at sunset and sunrise, they all looked depressed, as if being alive itself was an unbearable condition.

This implies that we are beings rooted in a sense of melancholy, a melancholy which is the natural result of being an individual thing. In order to be an individual thing, you need to have an illusion that you exist separately from and opposite to everything that has given rise to you. You need to be, in a sense, cut off, or have a feeling of being cut off. Then you say, 'I'm an individual'.

If the drop is part of the ocean, then you couldn't describe the drop as a drop. For the drop to be a drop, it has to be, in a sense, separated from the ocean. So, all things that are, are because they are cut off. This is particularly true for human beings because we are conscious beings with a claim to an autonomous, individual will. This sense of being an individual and having a separate will comes at the price of an experience of sadness.

Very often, people respond to this idea by saying that this experience isn't true for me. I think that is because people aren't entirely aware of their own experience of things. I do think that people have this experience. If people did not have this experience, there wouldn't be any need for compulsive behaviour. You can describe all compulsive behaviour as a desire to escape this primordial disquiet.

This is why we do things compulsively – why we binge watch TV, or play computer games, or smoke, or eat compulsively. It is because there's a sense of wanting to evade, escape, or be removed from this condition that paints a silent backdrop of disquiet to our beings. We all have this. We're just not necessarily aware of it.

I think the second thing that is true is that one of the things that one has to contend with on the path is that you are getting quieter. This creates the condition for you to become more aware of what is there on the inside. Our sense of disquiet becomes increasingly apparent as we grow. I would go so far as to say that the first sign of inner development isn't a growth in ecstasy; it's a growth in melancholy. It's a growth, in a sense, of alienation and depression.

It's not the practice that's alienating you. The practice is making you aware and is producing an inward gatheredness so that you become conscious of things that you weren't conscious of before. You start to be conscious of this sense of disquiet.

If this disquiet was an irremediable condition, if there was nothing for it, then it would indeed be a miserable thing to be a thing that is – whether you're human, or anything at all. If the price of being is a fundamental sense of sadness at being, then Allah SWT has played quite a cruel trick on us.

The extraordinary thing, particularly for human beings, is that we are able to hold onto two almost mutually exclusive experiences simultaneously. The first is this feeling of who we are, separated from the rest of existence. And the second is experiencing who we are, as part of the rest of existence. These two things aren't necessarily experiences that are mutually exclusive. They can exist simultaneously, and they can exist simultaneously in a continuum of intensity. If you think of it as a greyscale then, on one side of the scale, there's an absolute experience of alienation. And, on the other side of the scale, there is an absolute experience of continuity and connectedness, to the point where there's no experience of existing as a separate being at all. You've lost your identity completely. If you think of that as a continuum, then you can exist in a way where the degree to which either state is operative can change. So the more inwardly gathered you become, initially you become aware of this miserable condition of feeling alienated. But, over a period of time, you start to experientially feel yourself become connected with things outside of yourself. To be one with. To be informed by. To feel that that which you experience and you as the experiencer are part of a whole. You're not a separate being from it.

You're not sitting on this end of perception experiencing that on the other end of perception coming to you, but experience is one phenomenon. In the bubble of your being, there's that which is experienced. You're not separate from the world. You're not the observer of the world; the world and the observer are one thing. So what happens when you practice is, in the first instance, you become more aware of the melancholy. And then what happens is that incrementally you have these moments of quietude where you remember Him. Allah SWT says to us in the Qur'an that it is by the dhikr of Allah SWT that the heart becomes tranquil.

That means that the human heart is made to be in a state of disquiet unless it remembers. Remembers what? Remembers Allah SWT. And what is that memory? That memory is remembering that there's a unified field of being from which all things have come, which sustains, succours, and enables all things, including me. In other words, it is to remember that I'm not apart from Him, despite the fact that it appears that I'm apart from Him. When I remember this, I increasingly experience my connectedness with all that is. Then I increasingly find that my feeling of alienation and my feeling of disquiet and of melancholy is softened and quietened.

I think it is true then that you will have moments in your life where you are in sajda and you may just as well never come out of the sajda. Or you are sitting on your veranda, looking at a cloud, and all experiences of sadness, of loss, of disharmony, of alienation, and of melancholy are not there. They are not there because you are ecstatically entranced with the cloud, or with the touch of a child's hair, or with the look in a lover's eyes. There are an infinite number of these experiences. These experiences will grow to remind you that you are one with and not apart from.

In those experiences of one with and not apart from, you don't suffer the melancholy. It's not that the experience is somehow an anaesthetic or an ambrosia that deadens the truth. The melancholy is, like so many things, a half-truth because it is a response to an apparition.

If I threw a rubber snake at you and you got a fright, the fear is real, but the snake isn't. The melancholy is a response like the fear is, but it's the response to an illusory perception that I exist separately.

If you start truly seeing that separation is an illusion and you start giving yourself the opportunity to have experiences where you can demonstrate to yourself that the perception of existing separately is an illusion, then there will not be an experience of melancholy.

May Allah SWT grant us nearness to Him,
May He grant us annihilation in Him,
May He grant us death before we die.

Chapter 29

PETTY TYRANTS AND THE PATH

Discourse 29: 8 October 2020

Bismillah ar-rahman ar-raheem

In the Personal Excellence Programme that we did online this week, the Toltec device of the petty tyrant caused quite a stir. I had a number of people wanting a second pass at this idea because it seemed to them like a celebration of victimhood. That you just roll over and play dead and allow yourself to become the soccer ball of people, particularly of objectionable and difficult people.

In fact, nothing could be further from the truth. The first usefulness of the petty tyrant as a device is that it allows us to get a sense of detachment with regard to our requirements of people. It allows us to detach from our conditional motive. When somebody misbehaves to the extent that it upsets us, our being upset is the measure of the degree to which we require some sort of reciprocity from that person, at least the reciprocity of good behaviour. And when the person does not behave in an appropriately reciprocal manner, we believe that we are entitled to be outraged and upset.

You are always entitled to be outraged and upset, although that is not particularly constructive or useful. It doesn't matter who the person is, you are sweating the small stuff. The reason why Allah SWT puts impossible people in our lives is so that we can stop making people so significant. Everywhere you turn is the face of Allah SWT. So, wherever you turn, the totality of what is confronting you is His face. A face talks.

In any moment that you're in, He is giving you the next message. He is asking you, 'So what do you think about this?'. There is no stasis in His universe. How He has made something from nothing, how He has made

126

matter from exploding energy, solar systems from matter, and living things from dead things indicates that there is a deeply evolutionary drive to how He has created this theatre.

Rumi said that. He presaged Darwin for centuries. Allah SWT uses progression as an exploration of His own nature. He uses the same principle in your life, which means that He uses every moment that you are alive as an opportunity for you to progress in knowing Him. It is an opportunity to become bigger than yourself, transcend yourself, and to grow.

In any given moment, you can engage the moment on the basis of the intent to take, or the intent to give. When you engage in the moment on the basis of the intent to take, that which confronts you will dominate you. The rule is simple: if you want something from the other, the other has power over the self. Whenever you feel stuck, whenever you feel cornered, whenever you have any sense of victimhood about you, don't look at the person who is victimising you. Use that feeling as an opportunity to explore what you want from the person. It is your expectation that is creating the experience. You are your own jailer.

We know that the moment you engage the situation on the basis of what you are contributing, the situation loses its hold on you because you are able to let loose. You transcend the situation, and you grow. Your life is never retrogressive. It's either static or progressive. You are either stuck because you are dealing with it on the basis of your expectations, or you are growing.

We have also discovered that your capacity to act on the basis of what you could be giving is based on a perceptual skill. The first perceptual skill you need to learn is to put human beings back in their place. We give them disproportionate significance. Twenty years ago, my sister said something to me that offended me deeply. I can sit on my veranda here, in beautiful sunshine, birds around, the fountain bubbling, and I am offended by something that was said to me 20 years ago.

It is like having a broken tooth and sticking your tongue in it to feel how painful it is. This is how we are. We take unpleasant experiences, and particularly unpleasant experiences we have had with people, and we put them into completely disproportionate relief. It is as if I take that event and stick my nose up against it so closely that everything else disappears.

Is it not interesting that one of the ideas of gaining perspective is about standing back from, or gaining an elevated view? Going up on a mountain so that you can gain perspective. Stand away from the thing. People only upset you because you have your nose right up against what they did. Allah SWT has put impossible people in your life so that you can learn to disengage your face.

Learn to step back and not get so engaged in the tit for tat drama of people having to reciprocate your good behaviour. You can never reciprocate what you have been given by other people. If, from this day forward, every other person on the planet treated you with utter disregard and contempt, your suffering would not reciprocate the blessing that other people have already bequeathed to you for you to be here now. Why should anyone treat you as anything more than dirt? If you have this take on things, you have a deeply unshakable rock that you stand on. Because you no longer require other people to dance the dance with you.

Allah SWT puts these impossible people in our lives so we can learn to step back. When you step back, you are also forgoing the outcome and giving up control. Who takes over when you forgo control? Khairul raziqeen: the best of providers. Khairul makireen: the best of planners. The moment you stop coming to your own defence, He comes to your defence. What is required of you is not to act right, it is to see right. And seeing right means that you recognise that He is indeed your benefactor and your ally in the most surprising ways. This is particularly true when you allow Him to deal with impossible people in your life. And how do you allow Him to do so? You step back. You disengage. You become inwardly gathered. You become curious about the drama, rather than getting hooked into the drama. Your petty tyrant is the final proof that He will give you that He is your benefactor and your ally.

Carlos Castaneda said that there is nothing that tempers your spirit more than impossible people in positions of authority over you, particularly when they have the absolute prerogative of life and death over you. These people are the best because you cannot come to your own defence. If you allow yourself some patience to step back, to disengage, you will see the most extraordinary things. Things will change amazingly. The most irresolvable conflicts resolve themselves. And not necessarily in your or in that person's interest, but in a transcended interest that supersedes both. There is only one planner. Sometimes the thing that you want is not a good thing.

The further you go along this journey, the more you will recognise His hand in everything that happens to you. You will recognise His hand even in your own misbehaviour. You will recognise that the only reason why you have been made is to be amazed at Him. He is like a magician playing party tricks, moment by moment. That sense of amazement of the child at the magician's show is why we are alive.

He is waiting to delight you, but He can't show you the trick if you interfere. When you look in the hat, there is no party trick. He can only show the party trick when you allow yourself to be the audience.

Contrary to what people think, this capacity to put yourself in the audience and to forgo the outcome is not an act of cowardice or weakness. It takes the noblest qualities in you to have the restraint to do that - to not collapse in self-pity, to not rally to your own defence and fight back, to allow yourself to have a sense of humour about what is happening and to step back. This is the greatest act of fortitude. It is the greatest act of patience. It is the greatest act of courage.

A weak man comes to his own defence. When you come to your own defence, you are trying to control an outcome, and any attempt to control an outcome is an attribute of weakness. Any attribute which is the opposite of control is an attribute of power. It is the response of one who does not need to defend himself. That is power. The attempt to dominate and control others is not power. It is a weakness. Because it is rooted in fear.

Because the device of the petty tyrant is sometimes unpalatable, I strongly recommend that you are patient with this idea. It has been one of the most important tools of my own journey. There is nothing better for your growth than to be stuck face-to-face with an impossible person who is driving you to distraction.

May Allah SWT grant us nearness to Him,
May He grant us annihilation in Him,

May He grant us death before we die.

Chapter 30

FORGOING YOUR SENSE OF COMFORT
Discourse 30: 27 February 2022

Bismillah ar-rahman ar-raheem

The Rasul (s.a.w.s.) said he only came to perfect good character. Our entire endeavour, everything we do, is about becoming human beings who approximate good character. We say 'approximate' because it is naïve to believe that any human being can be held to an absolute standard. This is because humans are relative creatures. I would therefore invite you to consider everything that I am going to say about this matter in a spirit of compassion. It is easy to articulate or call on an ideal. It is a whole other matter to live your life by an ideal. In fact, when you have too many rules, when you script things too tightly, you get things wrong in big ways. You open yourself to the deeper problem of pride. We say that if you don't err in the small things, you will err in the big things.

Nevertheless, the matter I would like to pick up this evening relating to adab - courtesy and good character - is the understanding that one of the ways of describing courtesy is that it is doing the right thing at the right time. Part of doing whatever we do well is to do it at the right time. As Muslims, we know that going to the bathroom has its place and time, and we have a particular understanding of what cleanliness is and what you do in that context. Everything has its place and its time.

We also know that a Muslim's life is punctuated by salat, and you are enjoined to do salat in congregation. The Qur'an is full of references of Allah SWT indicating that success comes to those who establish salat and zakat. Establishing it means you institute it as a practice done by people, together. That is establishing it.

You can't do salat together if everyone does salat on their own time. It means that one of the rules of getting this thing right is that you do salat when everybody does salat. You come at the right time. You don't saunter in after the second or the third rakaat. This is not appropriate.

So why is it that we should have this tyrannical requirement that you should inconvenience yourself so that you can be in the saf at the same time as your brother fuqaraa' here at the Zawia? It is because all these practices are about forgoing. They are all about forgoing our own agenda for the agenda of the Rabb.

In any situation that you are in, there is what is comfortable for you, what is in your immediate self-interest, and there is what Allah SWT wants from you. This translates into the rule that in any situation, you can either give attention to what you want to get, or you can give attention to what you could give.

This giving is not just giving to other people. Clearly, it is giving to the best of your understanding of what it means to give to your Rabb. Your Rabb has required you to do salat with other people at the same time, which means you get there at the right time. It means you are in the saf at the time that the iqaama starts. You don't impose your slovenliness on everyone else by coming in the middle of salat. That is disrespectful and inappropriate.

This does not suggest that one sometimes gets it wrong, that you forget, or that you get caught up in something else and become late. It does not mean that sometimes one may not oversleep. We are all human beings. We understand this. But there is a difference between it happening on occasion and it happening routinely. This should not be the routine in the Zawia.

In the Zawia, not one of us is important enough to not be in the salat at the right time. This is because every one of us is fundamentally and irrevocably insignificant. A proper human being knows he is not here to be significant; he knows he is here to grant and witness significance. A person whose habit is to grant and witness significance does not think that they have license to behave as they like.

Punctuality is a very important thing. Without punctuality, there cannot be adab. The idea of adab without punctuality is nonsense.

There is this constant grinding, 'Ah! There is the adhaan again! I have to just drop what I am doing to get my wudhu', or even 'I take longer than everyone else to get my wudhu, I have to set my alarm 15 minutes earlier'. This constant grinding, this constant forgoing, this constant frustration of the little things which we are trying to do on an ongoing basis - our own little agendas - is exactly what this path is about.

That irritation and the cumulative effect of the small giving up is what produces a Muslim. The word Islam means submission. A Muslim is one who has submitted, one who truly submits. This is a person who practices submission by constantly working on forgoing what is comfortable, forgoing what is in your interest, forgoing for what is required of you in the situation.

This is also consistent with not taking your own sense of discomfort, your own sense of pique, and your own sense of being thwarted too seriously. The moment you feel that you have been in some way demeaned or you have some experience of a condition that does not suit you, you are enjoined to patience. Patience means that you do not take your own sense of discomfort seriously.

We sit in the morning for our morning muraaqaba meditation, and you have an itch, and you scratch the itch, and you fiddle and fuss. This suggests that you are taking your own sense of discomfort seriously. The reason why you are required to sit still and not fiddle and fuss is so that you can forgo your sense of comfort and not react to things that are uncomfortable. How do you propose to be patient with the big calamities of your life if you can't sit still for twenty minutes? How do you propose to deal with the real tests that are so extreme that they break your sense of self if you cannot deal with an insect crawling over your hand?

In fact, what you should be doing when you have something crawling over your hand is to use it as an exercise to prepare you for a time when you supremely don't come to your own defence. One way of understanding fanaa fillah is having an experience of such extremity that it shatters your sense of who you think you are, and you still do not come to your own defence. The moment you come to your own defence, you are reinvigorating this idea of an independent existence.

We are here to be washed, folks. That is what we are in the Zawia for. Washing in the first instance means we are subordinate to the basic requirements. These are not requirements that are set by me or by the tariqa; these are requirements set by your own deen. We all know that salat is more beneficial in jamaat. We all know that jamaat has a starting time called the iqaama. These are not mysteries.

May Allah SWT grant us nearness to Him,
May He grant us annihilation in Him,
May He grant us death before we die.

Chapter 31

OVERLOOKED TREASURE
Discourse 31: 2 October 2021

Bismillah ar-rahman ar-raheem

One wonders sometimes what the purpose of frailty is. We had so many experiences of frailty in the recent past, with people close to us either getting very ill or passing away. It seems as if one experiences these things as a curse, as an affliction. I was commenting to my son Muhammad today on the things I can't see anymore that I used to be able to see quite clearly. One has this sense of decline.

It occurs to me that one of the things that becomes apparent when you suffer affliction and discomfort is how much we take for granted. You don't realise something is working until it stops working. One takes one's eyesight for granted until you suddenly recognise that you cannot see things you used to be able to see. If you have a sore back, you suddenly realise just how much you take lying comfortably in bed for granted. When you have a lack of energy, you realise how much you take your normal vitality for granted.

It occurs to me that affliction is a reminder of the blessing that is there, the blessing that we don't normally recognise. We only recognise that we had something when it gets taken away from us. It occurs to me that this is the story of the human condition.

We all came from a place where we were one, united with Him, floating in an experience of transcendent bliss and delight. Then we were thrown into exile, into this world of affliction and struggle. We can ask, 'Why did this happen to us? Why were we thrown into exile? Why were we given this experience of being in this world where suffering is a foregone conclusion?'.

Maybe it is so that we can recognise the value of what was there. We will again recognise what was there when we go back to it because we assert,

inna lillahi wa inna ilayhi raji'uun

we have come from Allah SWT and we will return to Allah SWT

We will recognise the bliss and the ecstasy which is our fundamental nature, and which is the nature of existence.

Exile has a purpose. The purpose of exile is homecoming. Affliction has a purpose. The purpose of affliction is transcending the affliction. The purpose is to recognise the treasure that was overlooked. It was overlooked because it was taken for granted. We overlook the treasure of our existence. We overlook and take it for granted until we are brought to a time of alienation and separation. This produces a sense of appreciation for what is there.

There can be no other reason for existence. What is the purpose of the One who has all light and all bliss to create this state which is an apparently fallen state? A state of suffering and affliction. It can only have one purpose and that is to be a vantage point from which the perfection that sits at the root of things can be recognised, affirmed, and borne witness to.

This way of looking at things enables a lot of patience for me. Certainly, patience with my own sense of frailty and affliction. You don't know what health is until you've had illness. You don't know what joy is until you've had sorrow. You don't know what ecstasy is until you have had absolute depression. You know the thing by its opposite.

Shaykh Ali al Jamal said this directly. He said, 'The meaning of a thing is hidden in its opposite'. Without this, the world of the paradoxical and the contradictory experience would not be possible.

There is a naivete to our way of looking at things where we only want the light to win. Well, if only light won, you would be blind. Imagine, if the only thing you ever saw was white, then you could not see form. If it was not for darkness and shade, there would be no form. You would be blind.

This clumsy way of looking at things, where we want a utopian universe where everything works and everyone is happy, is naïve. It is not how Allah SWT has made this place. Why would He then speak of jihad, of the struggle, if it was not for the fact that this is a place of struggle?

This also gives us a license to be patient and compassionate with the frailty of others. In my experience, very few people set out to do that which is fundamentally diabolical. We misbehave because we are driven by things that are deeper than that which we have conscious control over. Once we recognise that in ourselves, we can recognise that in somebody else. We can be a bit more compassionate when we see them acting out their devils. The shadow. The dark.

We recognise that without that shadow, without that dark, there isn't a story. There isn't a human story. We have been expelled from the garden. We have been thrown into a world of struggle. This is true. Maybe that fallenness is the plan. In fact, it cannot be otherwise. Maybe Shaytaan himself plays a role for us. If we did not have the adversary, where would be the struggle?

And so, we can even grant him his place in the greater scheme of things. With all the suffering, we can still look back at the entire drama of existence and say: 'Which of these blessings will you deny?'.

May Allah SWT grant us nearness to Him,
May He grant us annihilation in Him,
May He grant us death before we die.

Chapter 32

Burn-Out: An Intent Problem

Discourse 32: 18 September 2021

B ismillah ar-rahman ar-raheem

During the week, I was driving to the mine on a rare client visit, and I had a useful conversation with my wife, Anna. It concerned a reflection of how I experienced going to that client in the past. I told her that I used to find it very draining, and I was trying to understand why. This led to an exploration of the idea of burnout, which is a very common phenomenon among people today, particularly people who work in corporate jobs.

People with corporate jobs often get very stressed and may even hit a wall where they are no longer able to work. This is a clinically recognized illness. It is called burnout and is regarded as a disease. It can knock people over for years and be a very unpleasant and debilitating experience.

It struck me, though, that some people can work very hard for extended periods of time, be as sleep-deprived as somebody else, and yet they do not get burnout. Why do some people get burnout and other people don't? It occurs to me that this has less to do with the work itself and more with what goes on, on the inside, and with one's intent patterns.

Burnout is an intent problem. The root of the problem lies in the idea of resources. The unfortunate development in modern English is that we have become used to thinking of the world and other people as resources. And if you use something as a resource, you will consume it. If you start mining a mineral resource, you use it up. When you frame your understanding of something as a resource, you will exhaust it.

The problem with all conditional motives is that when you are doing something from a conditional point of view, you are turning yourself - the one who is doing it - into a resource. A resource is something you use to get something. The implication is the following: if I do something to get something else, I am doing the doing. I, myself, am the resource that I am using to get the outcome that I want. The degree to which I treat myself as a resource to get an outcome is the degree to which I will deplete myself and burn myself out. I literally consume myself.

The structure of conditional motive makes the doer the thing that is being consumed in order to achieve something. This becomes really obvious when you think about basic things. How is it that on one day you could find a particular activity completely exhausting and, on another day, you find it nourishing? Walking, for example.

There are a number of places in the country where I have routinely walked up the same mountain. I find it fascinating that one day you could walk up the mountain and you could experience that walk as unmitigated hell. You suffer walking up the mountain; you are having to lug your carcass up the mountain.

When you are walking like that, to get to the top of the mountain, you stumble over every rock, walk through every bush, getting yourself injured and bruised because all your attention is on the top of the mountain. You are so purely concerned with getting to the goal, to the top, that you experience the rest of what is between you and the top as a hurdle that you have to get yourself over. When you are doing something to get there, it implies a discourtesy to the immediate, to what is in front of you, because you are pushing your way through it.

There is another way to walk up the mountain, which is to walk in order to enjoy the walk. That means your motive has inverted. I am not walking to get to the top of the mountain; the top of the mountain is my means to have a good walk. There is a shift in my attention from what I am trying to get to what I am doing or giving in the moment that I am in.

We all have had similar experiences. Sometimes you suffer from a journey, and, at another time, you find it pleasurable. You suffer the journey when you are in a hurry to get to the destination. Then the journey becomes an affliction and a misery that you have to endure to get to the outcome you want. You could enjoy the journey, give attention to the things as they pass you, and then, curiously, you may even get to the destination faster and you have not exhausted yourself in the process of getting there.

This thing of doing something to get somewhere else, giving in order to get, is the thing that exhausts us. It is not the journey. It is not the action or what sits in the world, in the outer, which is the depleting thing. What depletes you is what sits on the inside. It is the structure of your intent that depletes you. Anything that you do with intent to get something else will exhaust you in doing it.

Studying is an excellent example. Some people are good students because they love studying. They are nourished by studying. Other people suffer from studying because they are studying to pass an exam. That approach to studying exhausts and depletes them. It makes them hostile to the idea of studying.

In the life of the student, there is the studying, the examination, and the degree. If you use the examination as an opportunity to focus on your study so that you can study well, studying becomes pleasurable. However, if studying is the thing that you have to endure to get a degree, you deplete yourself when you study. It is not inconceivable for a student to get burnout.

This reflects poorly on how many parents deal with the education of their children. 'You must get a degree. You have to sell your life to the slavers so that you can become useful to the system.' And then we are surprised that we produce people who, in their mid-forties, have midlife crises, failed marriages, extreme stress problems, and hypertension.

We manufacture these people by these insane demands of having to comply. This disease of consuming yourself is not just doing things for selfish ends. If I reflect back on the period that I spent on that mine that I found very depleting, why was I going there? Well, there was a host of issues. I had the naïve belief that we could actually be useful to the client. So, there was an outcome for the client that I had in mind. I was also there because I had real financial responsibilities – I had to earn money. I was also there because I was concerned for the rest of the team that I was leading on that client site – that they wouldn't lose their work.

Most of these reasons were not actually selfish. They were quite benign. However, I was going to the mine to achieve an outcome. I was not going to the mine in order to enjoy the work.

This does not suggest that on this path, we bless hedonism. It has nothing to do with what you are actually doing. I therefore do not suggest you stop working. It means you should change your intent and your attitude to the work.

An example is cleaning the veranda in the Zawia. One way of cleaning the veranda is to do it to stay out of trouble. Then you will experience the sweeping as an onerous burden you have to get through in order to earn your keep in the Zawia. You could also explore how you could turn this into a pleasurable experience. Anything that you do in the spirit of doing it to do it well is a pleasurable experience. Don't just do things to get them done because that will exhaust you. Do things in order to do them well.

This is what we mean by sacralising a life. It means turning your life into a ritual. It means recognizing that everything has its own courtesy; you do the thing to do it well and eloquently. When you do things to get them done, you get consumed. When you do things to do them well, you get nourished.

If you experience the problem of feeling depleted by your work, that it is too much, of feeling that you can't carry on like this, it may be that you need to change the work that you do. However, open yourself to the possibility that most of the disease sits on the inside, on how your intent functions.

May Allah SWT grant us nearness to Him,
May He grant us annihilation in Him,
May He grant us death before we die.

Chapter 33

YOUR APPARENTLY MEDIOCRE LIFE
Discourse 33: 7 July 2021

Bismillah ar-rahman ar-raheem

Many of us experience our lives as trivial and mediocre. A common attribute of people on this path is that they are people who have discontentment with their day-to-day lives. They see their day-to-day lives as meaningless and insignificant. We have in us a desire to be rescued or redeemed from that sense of mediocrity and fallenness, of being in a lowly station. One of the sad mistakes we make is that we think that for this feeling of mediocrity and fallenness to be taken away, we somehow need to have a different life. We need different wealth, or we need to pray more regularly, or have a different car, or be accepted as moral or good by our peers.

Whatever our criteria are, we think that it is a world and a life other than the life that we have which represents a redeemed state. And that the state that we have is the fallen state. My experience is that this is not a helpful way of seeing things. On this path, you come back to the very ordinary life you sought to be redeemed from.

There is this description of a Buddhist, before enlightenment, cutting wood and drawing water and, after enlightenment, cutting wood and drawing water. This suggests that there is no external sign of whether a person is liberated. There is no external sign that this person is anything other than another struggling human being.

Each one of us is another struggling human being. We all have challenges concerning our wealth. We have challenges regarding our significance or our status in the eyes of others. What does change as you grow is that you learn to recognise that this apparently fallen and mediocre life of yours is, in fact, so extraordinary, so astonishing, that you do not need to be redeemed from it. It itself is the answer to itself.

That very cup of coffee that you have every day is a miracle, and to appreciate that single cup of coffee properly is to have lived a whole life well. You don't need to find a life, other than the life that you have. You don't need to change your world or to change yourself. You don't need to reinvent yourself, change your proportion of body fat to muscle, learn another language, and wear different clothes.

The change that is required is a perceptual change. It is the ability to recognise that what you have is already enough. That gratitude is the source of imaan. Unbelief or kufr is not just described as denying that Allah SWT exists, it is also described as ingratitude. That suggests that imaan, a redeemed state of being and of faithfulness, is one which is rooted in appreciativeness and gratitude.

This invokes the question: appreciativeness and gratitude for what? It is gratitude for that which you have. Whatever you see as part of your fallen state - whether it is poverty, a lack of education, a lack of health, a lack of opportunity, not being fit enough, not being attractive enough - your redemption does not come from having that thing fixed or changed for you. Your redemption comes from recognising that this very thing is actually extraordinary and that you need nothing other than it.

What you have now - the state that you have now, the financial status you have now, your popularity now, the home that you have now, the food that you eat, the clothing that you wear - you need none other than that. That in itself has enough blessing in it which, if you apprehended it for what it is, would keep your heart overflowing with a song of gratitude.

It is a heart that overflows with a song of gratitude that is the redeemed state. The redeemed state is not one of being rescued from the situation that you are in. Being redeemed means recognising that the situation that you have is one which is stupendous and one that deserves your gratitude. The change that produces the redeemed state is not an outer change, it is an inner change. It is an inner change that is radically concerned with gratitude. Our fallenness is rooted in our resentment and our redemption is rooted in our gratitude.

This path is not about becoming the stranger, the mystic, the foreigner, or the wanderer for whom normal life seems demeaned and demeaning. This path is about learning to discover the miraculous and the enchanting in the everyday. In the minutiae of everyday life. In the ordinary. Nothing is significant other than what you grant significance. Nothing is demeaned but for you having demeaned it. And this must be true for your own life. If you recognise that your life is significant, it is significant. If you consider your life to be one of fallenness that requires redemption, then that's what it is.

May Allah SWT grant us the gratitude to discover the gratitude in the ordinary.

May He grant us nearness to Him, annihilation in Him, and death before we die.

GLOSSARY

Adab - good manners, courtesy, respect, and appropriateness.

Adhaan - the Islamic call to prayer.

Akhira - the afterlife.

Alhumdullilah - all praise be to God.

Al-hayy - the living, the alive, the everlasting; one of the ninety-names of God.

AllahuAkbar - God is the most great.

Ar-rahman ar-raheem - the most compassionate, the most merciful.

Aml as-salihaat - doing good works.

Ana al-haqq - literally, 'I am the truth.' A statement attributed to the Persian mystic Mansur al-Hallaj (d. 922), who is said to have uttered these words as an expression of his spiritual station. Al-Hallaj was later executed purportedly on account of this statement.

Aya (singular) **ayat** (plural) - sign; a verse of the Qur'an.

Baqaa' - subsistence or permanency in God.

Bismillah ar-rahman ar-raheem - in the name of God, the most Compassionate, the most Merciful.

Dars - spiritual teaching, lesson.

Dhikr - remembrance, invocation, or glorification of God

Deen - derived from the term *dayn* meaning debt, or the debt that humanity has towards God; often translated as religion.

Du'a - a prayer of invocation, supplication, or request.

Dunya - the temporal world and its earthly concerns and possessions.

Faqeer (singular) **Fuqaraa'** (plural) - the one who is poor and needy towards God, knowing his own insignificance in the face of the Majestic, all Significant.

Ghazwa - A battle or raid against non-Muslims.

Halaal - that which is lawful according to Islamic law.

Hadith - a saying of the Prophet Muhammad (s.a.w.s)

Hijra - the Prophet Muhammad's migration along with the early Muslim community from Mecca to Medina in 622 CE in order to escape persecution.

Imaan - belief or faith.

Kaafir (singular) **kuffaar** (plural) - one who covers the truth, an unbeliever.

Khairul raziqeen - the best provider of sustenance.

Khairul makireen - the best of planners.

Kufr - covering up or denial or suppression of the truth.

Fanaa fillah - the annihilation of the ego or self in God.

Fi sabeelallah - in the way of God. Performing action purely for the pleasure of God, as an act of devotion or worship.

Furqaan - criterion or discernment; another name for the Qur'an.

Haqq - deep truth or reality; commonly used in Sufism to refer to God; one of the ninety-nine names of God.

Inna lillahi wa inna ilayhi raji'uun - indeed we come from God and to Him we return; a phrase that is often said on hearing of someone's death.

Iqaama - the second call to prayer, given immediately before the congregational prayer begins.

Janna - paradise.

Jamaat - prayer in congregation.

Jihad - struggle; exertion. The constant and vigilant inner struggle against the nafs or lower self is described as the greater jihad, while the struggle and fight against the enemies of Islam is known as the lesser jihad.

Khalwa - solitude; in Sufism, isolation in a solitary place for spiritual exercises.

Kun fa yakuun - 'Be and it is'; a phrase oft repeated in the Qur'an, this was God's command that preceded the creation of the world and also expresses the ease with which God can actualize the impossible.

La ilaaha illallah - there is no god but God.

Masjid - mosque.

Muhajireen - the early converts to Islam and the Prophet Muhammad's advisors and relatives, who emigrated from Mecca to Medina during the Hijra in 622 CE.

Mu'min - the believer or the one with faith.

Muraaqaba - Sufi meditation.

Mureed - disciple of a Sufi shaykh; seeker, aspirant, Sufi disciple; literally, one desiring to be guided on the spiritual path by a teacher.

Murabitun - a movement led by Shaykh Abdul Qadir as-Sufi.

Musalla - literally, 'a place for prayer'; prayer mat.

Nasrallah - the help of God.

Nafs - the self or ego; in Sufism often used in the negative sense of 'lower self'.

Niyya - intention.

Qawwali - Sufi devotional music.

Rabb - Lord.

Rabb al-'aalameen - Lord of the worlds.

Rakaat - a single unit of prescribed movements and supplications in prayer.

Riba - usury.

Ruh - the soul.

Sadaqa - a voluntary charitable act.

Sabr - referring to patience, endurance, and self-restraint.

Saf - rows in congregational prayer.

Sajda - bowing down in prostration; one of the postures during ritual prayer.

Salafi - a Muslim scholar or activist who considers the period of the Prophet and his companions as the exclusive source of religious norms in Islam.

Salat - formal ritual prayer offered by Muslim five time daily.

Sawm - fasting.

s.a.w.s. - an abbreviation for **sallallahu 'alayhee wa sallam**: may the blessings of God be upon him and peace. These words are spoken after the hearing or reading the name of the Prophet Muhammad.

Shadhiliyya - Sufi order founded on the teachings of Abu al-Hasan al-Shadhili (d. 1258).

Shaheed - martyr.

Shaytaan - evil spirit, demon, devil.

Shaykh - an elder, religious scholar, or Sufi master.

Shirk - Idolatry, polytheism, or the association of God with other deities.

SWT - an abbreviation for **subhanahu wa ta'ala**: glorious and most high is God.

Subhanallah - glory be to God.

Tariqa - the Sufi path; this term is also used to describe a Sufi group or order.

Tasawwuf - Sufism, the inner dimension of Islam.

Thawab - reward, in the afterlife.

Umma - the past and present community of the Prophet Muhammad.

Wali - Helper or friend; in Sufism, friend of God.

Waswasa - whisperings.

Wudhu - a cleansing ritual or ablution that is an important part of purity and cleanliness in Islam before performing worship.

Zakat - that which purifies. It refers to the charity required of Muslims in Islam.

ABOUT THE AUTHOR

Etsko Schuitema is a Sufi teacher from the Darqawi-Shadhiliyya tariqa, where he is known as Shaykh Ebrahim. He runs the Zawia Ebrahim, a Sufi spiritual retreat centre in Gauteng near Johannesburg, South Africa, which he founded in 2000.

Born into a Catholic family, Shaykh Ebrahim had a curiosity about the inner reality from a young age. During his youth, he explored multiple spiritual traditions until he became Muslim in 1981. Soon after accepting Islam, he gravitated towards circles of dhikr and the path of tasawwuf. In 2000, Shaykh Ebrahim received his idhn or chain of transmission in the Darqawi-Shadhiliyya tariqa from Shaykh Mustafa Bassir (d. 2006) of Morocco (may Allah bless his soul).

He is also the founder of the Schuitema Group, a business transformation consultancy dedicated to the enhancement of human excellence based on the Care & Growth™ model.

To find out more about the Zawia Ebrahim, please visit: *https://zawiaebrahim.com/*

To find out more about the Schuitema Group, please visit: *https://www.schuitemagroup.com/*

ompliance